Historic
Towns of Australia

Historic Towns of Australia

Philip Cox   Wesley Stacey

Lansdowne

First published 1973 by
Lansdowne Press
a division of Paul Hamlyn Pty Limited
176 South Creek Road, Dee Why West, Australia 2099
2nd impression 1974
3rd impression 1978
© P. Cox & W. Stacey 1973
Typeset by Monotrade Pty Ltd, Melbourne
Printed and bound in Hong Kong
Designed by Derrick I. Stone
National Library of Australia Card Number and
ISBN 0 7018 0184 0
The Publishers wish to thank Trans-Australian
Airways for travel assistance given to the authors.

12921

Contents

Authors' Note

This book was written to bring attention to some of the few remaining country
towns in Australia which still have the majority of their nineteenth century buildings intact.
Be they Georgian, Victorian or Edwardian, it is important that these buildings combine to
form an urbanscape evocative of the past and its life style. These towns are precious for they
are rare. Some towns have been mutilated through meaningless laws —
particularly in New South Wales (and no doubt in other States)—which compel owners of
buildings to effect immediate demolition of their verandahs. By this stupid law our whole
architectural and urban heritage has been threatened, and in some cases has almost
disappeared. To walk through towns such as Mudgee and Yass in New South Wales, today,
is to walk through towns stripped of their glory. Where once verandahs with delicately
turned columns graced Georgian buildings or, in Victorian examples, cast iron lace threw
dappled shadows across the pavement, these buildings now lie bare, stripped naked—mutilated.

It is hoped that the Department of Tourism may take note. Perhaps even the
Commonwealth Government with its Department of the Environment may realise the
potential of the towns contained in this book and proclaim them worthy of preservation and
assist them financially.

If these towns are to survive, a proper plan of preservation needs to be drawn up. It may
even be dangerous for these towns, in their present state, to have increased tourism before
such plans are made as success may breed new buildings, such as motels and hotels, which
may be insensitive to the architectural character of the town and destroy the very
urbanscape and life style for which they are important.

Europe, and now America, have both realised the potential of their villages and towns.
They have pride in their restoration—they treat them as a treasure of architectural and social
history. It is all very well preserving individual examples of architecture in the city and

country—but that is not good enough; they will never give the complete sensation of the life style of a community. We need to do more—we need to preserve total environments: trees, buildings, streetscapes, townscapes—nothing can be treated in isolation.

We hope this book will provide interest in these towns both visually (from an architectural and planning point of view) and historically.

Philip Cox
Wesley Stacey
1973

Acknowledgements

We wish to thank all the Shires included in this book who have assisted in providing us with information. In particular, Mr Eric Nicholas of Philip Cox, Storey and Partners Pty Ltd who gave considerable assistance in the research of the book and Louise Cox who helped check it. We gratefully acknowledge the assistance and the permission to reproduce extracts provided by all State libraries. In particular the Mitchell Library in New South Wales, the State Library of Tasmania, the Oxley Library in Queensland, the Western Australian Public Library and the South Australian Public Library. We have drawn heavily on previous articles, tours, and projects by many authors more familiar with some of the histories and these are acknowledged separately in the bibliographies of each town.

We thank Mr Stancombe of Tasmania who so kindly wrote the text for Evandale, Tasmania, and Mr Hal Missingham and Mr Richard Woldendorp who supplied photographs of Broome.

We thank Mr John Toon, Senior Lecturer in Town Planning, Sydney University, for consenting to write the Preface to this work.

Preface

Australia is a nation of planned towns. There is barely a single settlement that is not planned; yet it is a general truth that Australian towns are dull, repetitive and lacking in personality or 'image'.

It is equally true that most of the world's towns and cities are also planned; yet towns and cities elsewhere are rarely dull or repetitive and many have quite dramatic images.

Why is this so?

The difference lies, in part, in the interpretation and application of the concept of town-planning—who plans? for whom? with what purpose?

The ancient urban cultures—the Middle-East and China—evolved from a long process of interaction between man and his environment. Town building was invariably woven about established social organisation and rituals and subject to widely accepted and understood conventions. Cultural differentiation between districts or regions was inevitable since inter-communication was limited; there emerged a wide range of language, symbolism, belief and social structure. The villages, towns and cities that emerged as a result of these cultures were equally varied. Yet each was a deliberate creation—a planned settlement.

The aboriginal culture in Australia, as ancient as the great urban cultures, never created cities. Yet the sacred grounds and ceremonial gathering places were in fact embryonic cities; in theory these symbolic places may have evolved into an urban form that would be recognised by western eyes. Although not readily identifiable in their pre-urban state, most aboriginal symbolic grounds have natural characteristics—a sense of place—that are comparable with the Acropolis at Athens or the Forum at Rome, both of which locations are known to have been significant for many hundreds of years prior to their reaching the historic form that is familiar today.

Most aboriginal symbolic places have sadly disappeared under the ruthless process of colonisation. Yet it is possible to hypothesise that these places would have exhibited characteristics that are commonly found elsewhere; they would, for instance, be adjacent to a reliable water source; they would probably have been selected with an acute awareness of local micro-climate since the Aboriginals relied little on clothing or structures to modify climate. The symbolism of place could have been expressed in many ways; the most common would probably be places that gave visual command of a territory or, perhaps, a waterway; others may have been places of convergence where people drawn from a hinterland could readily gather. It is likely that these places would have had some permanence and be protected from inundation, erosion and other natural hazards.

Indeed, aboriginal culture had the characteristics necessary for an 'urban' culture, albeit fairly primitive. That the Aboriginals never crossed this threshold is most likely due to the incredible climatic vagaries of Australia. For a true urban culture to evolve depends upon the probability of an individual, or group, being able to exercise control over people and resources—essentially food but also including commodities of symbolic and functional value. The extreme climatic variations—floods, droughts and bushfires—combined with their unpredictability suggests that the level of available sustenance in any one location would have been highly variable; there are very few, if any, locations in Australia where one could confidently predict a permanent and reliable supply of food and water. Even modern urban Australia, with all its command of technology and resources, continually suffers from the same uncertainty. A typical example, repeated time and again by early explorers, is the wide divergence in assessment of particular locations; compare, for instance, Cook's and Phillip's assessment of Botany Bay.

Early colonisation suffered dreadfully on account of the inability to understand the new land —*Terra Australis Incognito*. The first settlers must have thought of the land in hateful and hostile terms.

All this Country as far as the eye can reach from very high Hills bears the most dreary barren appearance which can well be imagined. Nothing to be seen but ridge beyond ridge of Mountains cover'd with Trees and in many places with Rocks without a single visible interval of plain or Cultivable land (The Blue Mountains).

. . . *land still worse almost entirely overflow'd with floods* (Maralya).

. . . *sandy barren swampy Country* (Rockdale).

. . . *stony and apparently very barren* (Leppington).

In floods the water rises to the height of 50 feet perpendicular leaving Reeds etc. in the Trees (Nepean River).

. . . *A patch of good land* (Chatswood).

(All from Watkin Tench's narrative 1793).*

No doubt Tench's pessimism was counterbalanced by the optimism which is a recurring theme in the culture of Australia. Yet most must surely have regarded the environment as extremely hostile. Even the emerging global confidence of the British—epitomised by

---

* *Sydney's First Four Years* by Captain Watkin Tench with an introduction by L. F. Fitzharding (reprint); Angus and Robertson 1961.

Wesleys' comment 'I look upon the whole world as my parish'—must have been severely tried by such a coarse and uncompromising environment. How often must early settlers' thoughts have returned to the gentle climate and benign countenance of the home country.

British society in the late eighteenth century was both stable and confident. Parliament, untroubled by the monarchy, sought power, wealth and trade wherever the opportunity arose. Political power and wealth was spread through the upper echelons of society unlike elsewhere in Europe. Its legacies are the elegant Georgian squares of London, Craig's Edinburgh New Town and a few restrained country houses.

Wealth was sufficiently widely diffused through an expanding elite to create a market for fine-quality products—silk clothing, handsome furniture, elegant silverware and comfortable coachwork. Georgian artisans needed to innovate to meet new demands. Arkwright built his mill in 1768 in a bid to meet these demands. Wedgewood and countless others experimented with new techniques to create more goods more efficiently to satisfy the growing demand.

By 1800, the wealthy were content to live off income earned on capital; they were amused by Shelley and Beau Brummell at Bath. The innovators, the traders, the explorers were pegging out the world in the name of the Crown. An Empire was born.

The settlement of Australia was but a small and insignificant part of the emergent Empire. As elsewhere, settlement was directed towards exploitation of resources; in the case of Australia, an additional requirement was the accommodation of convicts. The entire process of empire building was directed by Parliament.

The early governors were agents of the Crown; they wielded absolute authority in all matters. The management expertise accumulated over two centuries was exercised in the exploitation of each new colony's resources. The refined taste and respect for law and order of the elite was married to the pragmatism and innovatory abilities of the artisans to carve out of the Australian environment a new appendage to the Empire. There was never any question that this could not be achieved. But it was no easy task.

The struggle between authority, with its desire to keep the process of settlement regulated and well-ordered, and the pragmatism of the innovators, with their desire to maximise every opportunity that occurred, has persisted throughout Australian history. If town building is any indicator whatever of that struggle then authority was never seriously undermined.

For the subdivision of a whole continent was laid out according to authoritarian rules.

Each village and each town was laid out in a standardised grid. The distances between each were carefully regulated and determined by transport facilities available. Towns and villages were spaced out in a ruthless geometric order. Land subdivision was regulated by a similar geometric order. Streets were standard widths and laid out on a grid pattern.

The standardisation and regularity of arrangement were the hallmarks of authority; each town was related in a hierarchical manner to Westminster. Sometimes particular sites were earmarked for a court house or a church, but generally towns were laid out as geometrical abstractions—in a similar manner to the Greek and Roman colonial towns that had been laid out some 2000 years previously.

A few early towns, like Parramatta and Windsor, did not conform to the pattern. Others, like Port Macquarie and Brisbane, had been laid out pragmatically as penal settlements but were re-organised to conform to the standard pattern. Sydney, despite repeated efforts, was never quite brought under control.

The whole purpose of the exercise was directed towards creating rural land holdings for agricultural purposes. The many hundreds of towns created within the pattern of rural subdivision were merely incidental to agricultural production—production that was linked to the demands of the British economy.

The greatest constraint to rural expansion was the difficulty of overland transport; there was a vain search for routes that connected hinterlands to ports. Until the introduction of railways, road transport was the only means of movement available. Numerous expeditions traversed the broken topography of the Great Dividing Range in search of good routes that would connect the inland agricultural areas with ports; '. . . it was a continual ascending and descending of the most frightful precipices, so covered with trees, shrubs and creeping vines that we frequently were obliged to cut our way through.' (Oxley's account of the descent from the dividing range to the Hastings River 1818).

Berrima, for instance, was at one time intended as a regional capital with a connection to Jervis Bay. Some such routes were developed and coastal ports played an important role up to the mid-nineteenth century. These coastal towns, some of which have since disappeared, were the more interesting because of their locational requirements. Even so, they did not depart radically from the authoritarian pattern.

The gold rushes and subsequent mining towns did not lead to any major innovations in town planning. Some, like Ballarat, Bendigo, Broken Hill and Gulgong, did acquire a splendid array of full-blooded Victorian buildings as a consequence of mining, but the town plans retained the characteristic grid.

Of all towns and cities laid out in the settlement period, only Adelaide is a radical departure. Laid out by Colonel Light in 1834, it is graced by a series of five squares in geometrical fashion around the central Victoria Square; the original lots were square acres and the grid structure has a marked east-west orientation. It is best known for its generous parklands surrounding the town subdivision. The nearby village of Glenelg, also laid out by Light, is a sensitively scaled village focused on a single square.

The location of all towns was strongly influenced by the availability of water; most were located adjacent to rivers and streams, or in estuarine situations. Generally, a well-drained position with moderate slopes was selected. Some of these locations have been subject to recurrent flooding, but that may be due more to the clearance of land for agricultural purposes than a fault in the original site selection.

It is interesting to contrast the siting of towns with the siting of homesteads. Many homesteads are located on middle slopes, or on minor prominences—situations that invariably reflect an intimate understanding of the local micro-climate; all too often towns are located in valleys and suffer from adverse micro-climate conditions such as cold air drainage, frost exposure and poor ventilation. Town locations were more often determined by strategic considerations (e.g. a river crossing point) than comfort. The orientation of streets was often inappropriate in terms of winds and sunlight. Such factors are usually only reflected in town plans that are evolved by local communities. Canberra is a rare example of a planned town that is well related to the local environment; it reflects the awesome insight and genius of Burley Griffin who had not even seen the site.

More typically, town layout did take into account local topographical eminences and variations. The most common device was the orientation of the principal street towards a topographical eminence. Albury, Cowra and Parramatta all reflect this characteristic. This theme is echoed magnificently in Canberra.

Town plans require buildings to make towns. The layout of Australian towns was not demanding in architectural terms. The cultural response to a hostile environment was to recreate home. The addition of verandahs—an early response to the climate—was the only variation to building forms that epitomised home. There are few examples of whole towns that reflect home. Oatlands, the epitome of a Kent village and Ross, redolent of East Anglia, are the best examples. Individual buildings that stand out are the court houses and the early homesteads. There are some examples of streets that have evolved a consistency of architecture adapted to Australia. Pall Mall, Bendigo; Naylor Street, Carcoar and Mayne Street, Gulgong are good examples. Yet, sadly, there are so few satisfying towns.

Innovation in Australian town planning has always been constrained by authority—even to the present time. A number of magnificent *beaux-arts* town plans were put forward in the early part of the twentieth century—mainly as speculative ventures; remnants of some of these can still be found at Bathurst or Albury, New South Wales. Griffin produced his pioneer 'radburn' plans at Castlecrag and Heidelberg; the major innovations occurred in suburban layouts around the capital cities and in the emerging holiday towns along the coast; challenging landscapes were modified, not always successfully. A few new towns like Griffith and Leeton departed from the traditional pattern.

Now, once again, government authorities have assumed wide powers that will influence town planning. The challenge facing these authorities is to avoid stultifying standardisation and to encourage an imaginative and humane approach to the planning of new urban environments. This challenge is very real for once towns are laid out they become one of the fixtures of a culture.

In Australia, the urban heritage is sadly stereotyped. If any lesson is to be learnt from history, it is that a more flexible and adaptive approach on the part of the authorities is necessary if town building is ever to achieve the distinction that is evident in other parts of the world.

John Toon
University of Sydney.
March 1973

Introduction

The final Mission of the city is to further man's conscious participation in the cosmic and the historic process. Through its own complex and enduring structure, the city vastly augments man's ability to interpret these processes and take an active formative part in them, so that every phase of the drama it stages shall have, to the highest degree possible, the illumination of consciousness, the stamp of purpose, the colour of love. That magnification of all the dimensions of life, through emotional communion, rational communication, technological mastery, and above all, dramatic representation, has been the supreme office of the city in history and it remains the chief reason for the city's continued existence. Lewis Mumford.

Sydney as the first settlement in Australia set the pattern for urban development. The story of its development, from a straggling collection of cottages around the Tank Stream, and its decline in importance as lands within the Cumberland Plain were opened up for grazing and agriculture, with emphasis on Parramatta as a more conveniently located agricultural centre, is well known. With the opening up of the Hawkesbury lands Sydney's importance once again grew.

The first attempt at town planning in Australia was Captain Phillip's proposal for street layout in 1792. In describing this proposal, Phillip stated that 'the principal streets are placed so as to admit a free circulation of air and are two hundred feet wide.' Unfortunately the plan which Phillip envisaged was not carried out. The luxuries of planning and civic grouping were dropped for expediency.

An official plan was produced in 1807 by the surveyor James Meehan under the instructions of Captain Bligh and this shows locations of the principal streets and the central area of Sydney very much as they are today. The layout shows Sydney as a military establishment, very much Government orientated, with many of the features of an establishment versus an underdog convict society. On this plan Fort Phillip is shown on the high ridge with the government windmills. This skyline can also be seen in the illustrations of Lycett in his early views of Sydney. High Street (now George Street) was the principal street and alongside were the military parade grounds and military hospital. Pitt Street was well defined as was Camden Street (now Elizabeth Street). The street pattern was irregular, especially around Sydney Cove where the Tank Stream entered the Harbour. The reason for this was probably the need for well reserves around the Tank Stream, and it was expedient to follow the established bush tracks which wandered around the trees and boulders of the sandstone terrain.

Government House, the seat of administration, was the focal point of this irregular pattern and stood just below the ridge which is now Macquarie Street, approximately on the corner of Bridge and Phillip Streets.

By 1822 Governor Macquarie found buildings had encroached on the street pattern reducing their width, and he arranged therefore to have the streets re-surveyed to establish a minimum sixty foot width. Macquarie was concerned with the overall form of the town and interested in the eventual creation of a plan fit for the capital of the colony. No doubt Macquarie was urged by his architect, Francis Greenway, who, in a letter to Macquarie in 1817 stated:

It will be necessary to have a plan of the town of Sydney in the first place. To lay down a plan for a town requires the greatest circumspection, however lightly it may be thought of by those who can have no just idea of it. To lay out streets upon proper intersecting in certain points would be very well were the ground as level as the paper on which you design it, but when the ground is irregular and full of hills and valleys it requires a very different treatment as buildings calculated for a level piece of ground would be ruin and madness to build upon another. There are very few buildings in the town at all designed or calculated for their situation nor will the town ever be regularly built or safe from fires and these dangers for many reasons until proper Regulations are made and regular designs for streets approved by your Excellency.

Greenway went on to discuss the various arteries and services necessary for the functioning of a town. He suggested that 'a proper conduit should be formed concentrating the springs in and about Sydney' as it was essential, in his opinion, 'to have a reasonable water supply and not rely upon wells.'

Sewers were also needed. 'A main sewer,' he said, 'should be made as another essential public undertaking and all persons building should be obliged to lead their drains to it in order to avoid numerous disgusting inconveniences in the future.' Greenway concluded his letter by saying that a 'well built town with every elegant public and private accommodation from your Excellency's well known desire would improve the colony.'

Sydney continued to grow in a more orderly fashion from Macquarie's time and reservations were made for the principal parks and open spaces. The racecourse (now Hyde Park), the Botanical Gardens and Macquarie Place, are a few examples of a more civic approach to planning at this time.

By 1848 Joseph Fowles in his *Sydney in 1848* could comment that:

Sydney occupies a space of more than two thousand acres. By the census taken in 1846, the number of houses in the city was seven thousand, one hundred.

The public institutions are numerous and flourishing. There are four banks of issue, the Bank of New South Wales, and the Commercial Bank, both colonial, and the Union Bank of Australia, and the Bank of Australasia, Anglo-Australian. We have an Australian Gas Light Company, an Australian Sugar Company, Sydney Fire Insurance Company, and a Sydney Marine Insurance Company. The Literary and Scientific Institutions are the Australian Subscription Library, the Mechanics' School of Arts, the Australian Museum, the Society for the promotion of the Fine Arts and the Floral and Horticultural Society. There are numerous Lodges of Free Masons and Odd Fellows and several Religious, Social and Benefit Societies.

The Joseph Fowles' description gives us an insight into the social structure of towns. Certainly human settlements of all ages are an expression of the aspirations and requirements of the societies which created them. Sydney in 1848 was at its Georgian zenith, a town rich in its aspirations, an orderly defined architectural expression of two-storied dwellings. The skyline was punctuated by the spires of St James Church and other religious edifices, not to forget the many windmills which lined the ridge of Millers Point.

There was no need in Australia to site towns upon hill tops for defence or to surround them with walls, or, in fact, to concentrate dwellings in a defence ring or square. The natives, although troublesome, were very little threat, and there were only isolated cases of attacks or assaults on any settlement. The physical characteristics of the land tended to sprawl and the towns adopted these same sprawling features.

The early land surveys were based upon the rectangular or gridiron pattern and this offered many advantages to a surveyor in opening up new territory to settlers. He could make new boundaries by extending existing survey lines and the lots so formed by a gridiron survey could be numbered and calculated easily in terms of land content.

Grid surveys began in Governor Brisbane's time when surveys of towns were instructed in 1821 and the same passion for rectangular order extended to the planning of towns by Governor Darling.

Darling published extensive regulations in the *Sydney Gazette* in May 1829 which emphatically laid down the future development of country towns in Australia and included:

1. *The streets, wherever practicable from the Nature of the grounds are to be made Rectilinear, and the*

cross streets are to be laid down at right angles to the main street.

2. *The width, to be reserved for main streets, is to be one hundred feet, consisting of eighty feet carriage way and a footpath, on each side of ten feet. In cross or inferior streets, width is to be eighty-four feet, that is a carriage way of sixty-six feet and a footpath on each side of nine feet.*

3. *Within the limits above mentioned, no steps or projections of any kind will be allowed.*

4. *The distance from the footpath in every street, at which all persons will be required to build, will be exactly fourteen feet, and the open space thus left is to be appropriated exclusively to open verandah, or such plantation as may be desired. The distance, therefore, between the opposite houses, will be one hundred and twenty-eight feet in the main streets, and one hundred and twelve feet in the cross or inferior streets.*

5. *With the view of preserving general continuity of line, the above mentioned space of fourteen feet, in front of the houses will be required to be enclosed with an open fence or where it may be desirable to have free Ingress and Egress as to shops etc. by posts, ten feet apart, etc.*

There was little agreement on the width of the main streets. Those army officers and settlers who had experienced colonial service in India argued that wide streets allowed the circulation of breezes in hot climate. Surveyor T. L. Mitchell preferred the narrow and shady streets of Spain where he had served in the Peninsular War. He stated 'a narrow street in a country subject to hot winds, dust and a scorching sun is rather desirable than otherwise'. In the light of events Mitchell's plan of a Mediterranean village was not carried on.

Darling's laws had a completely undesirable effect for future towns in Australia, the majority of which were laid out on the gridiron pattern without any heed for topography, soil condition, natural feature or view. On the examination of Mitchell's plan for Maitland, 1829, there are however, provisions for squares, the siting of important civic buildings on high spots. These subtleties were completely ignored in the majority of towns in New South Wales. When Braidwood was being surveyed as a town, the citizens showed greater sensitivity than the Government by requesting that reservations be made for open space in front of the Court House and other important buildings to give some civic dignity.

Melbourne was founded in 1835 and followed the traditional bold gridiron pattern with principal streets ninety-nine feet wide. Nothing more could have been expected as the plan was principally the work of Robert Hoddle who had laid out many towns in New South Wales in a similar fashion. In 1837 Hoddle was made the Surveyor-General of Victoria and was responsible for three chain-wide arterial roads leading into the city. These were originally intended as stock routes.

By contrast, Adelaide, founded in 1836, was constructed according to a plan devised by Colonel Light, the first Surveyor-General of South Australia. The plan is unique and sophisticated in many ways. Firstly a large reservation was held around the river for recreational purposes and this divided the city into two interesting sectors. The commercial sector of the city was designed on a gridiron pattern but with a difference. Instead of the customary boundary of street design and the lack of visual interruption, Light created a central square balanced in plan by four smaller squares. Around these were to be built the principal buildings. Surrounding the whole of the city was a green belt which confined and defined the growth of the city and was originally intended to check dispersed form. On the periphery of the city were five acre allotments for agricultural use. The plan predetermines, to a large extent, contemporary town planning principals and certainly advanced the best town planning theory of Georgian England. Nothing of this scale and magnificence was to be seen in Australia again until the planning of the National Capital by Walter Burley Griffin.

Towns in Australia were established for a variety of purposes. Some were ports for the collection of goods for shipment to other countries. Such towns were either inland ports on the great river systems such as Wilcannia, Bourke, Wentworth, Goolwa or sea ports— Sydney, Portland, Newcastle, Melbourne.

Most of the towns seem to have been created as centres for the great expansion which took place in the gold rush period 1850 to 1890. If by fortune these towns occurred in pastoral districts their chances of survival at a later date were good and many continued to flourish after the gold rush era. Others did not and these just perished. Towns in New South Wales such as Hill End almost vanished while a town like Gulgong, situated near the richer pastoral areas of Mudgee, continued to survive. Similar examples of this occurrence can be found in all States.

As transport needs changed so did the location and prosperity of many towns. The decline of the river traffic in New South Wales, Victoria and South Australia sounded the death knell to many towns along the river systems. With the growth of railways other towns grew.

Some towns were established as commercial centres for primary industry regions. Mostly these towns consist of a standard plan similar to Darling's gridiron plan of principal street with side streets playing a minor role. Within the town the most important architectural contributions were usually the hotels, which stood alone in size and importance, displaying the height of architectural fashion, embellishment and ostentation.

Following closely upon the hotels were the civic buildings, assuming the town enjoyed a certain status. The court house and post office were always treated with dignity and sobriety of expression by the government architects. Rarely is there a dose of flamboyance in style, rather the architectural designs depend upon mass and scale, or position within the town itself, for effect.

In strategic positions within the town churches were located, usually the Church of England which, because of its official position, occupied a choice site with a glebe. Most of the churches designed between 1850 and 1900 were neo-Gothic expressions of the vernacular and yet they were imbued with a vigour that classical examples seldom achieved. The Roman Catholic Church tended towards the more flamboyant and often lacked the refinement or dignity of the Church of England. By far the most simple and pure expression of ecclesiastic architecture is to be seen in the Presbyterian Church. Many fine examples of simple church architecture are to be found throughout the country. An example such as the Presbyterian Church at Evandale, set amongst the gum trees and surrounded by a picket fence, is one of the most excellent examples of civic and yet rural architecture in Australia.

The characters of country towns differ depending upon the geography, climate, soil, rainfall, aspect and topography which all play important roles, and each fashions the town in its own way.

The instant Australian character of towns is generally created by verandahed broad walks and in many ways they have similarities with the mid-western mining towns in America. In Australia the verandah had the additional function of keeping the sun off the building and in creating cool shadows across the building façade. The value of the verandah can easily be appreciated in the inland towns of Australia where summer temperatures soar well above 38° C. In addition to the physical properties, the verandah gave scope for decoration as well as additional display for sign writing, a sitting place for people, a place where clothes could be dried on the wet days, or a place where drinks could be taken in the summer months.

Towns were built from a variety of building materials—timber, brick or stone—depending on the availability of these natural resources. The mining towns tended to carry a temporary appearance with timber, no doubt resulting from the original canvas structure of the miner's tents, whilst agricultural or pastoral settlements usually started with more permanent structures. The Holtermann photographs of Hill End and Gulgong show this temporary nature of a mining town. A town like Beechworth in Victoria had its temporary timber buildings soon replaced by brick and stone and became a very proper town by the 1870s.

The early roofing material of most of the town buildings was timber shingles which was replaced by galvanised iron by the mid-nineties. Generally the iron was fashioned into a variety of roof shapes either pitched, gabled or hipped. In many examples of commercial architecture the roof was hidden by a large parapet which was either stepped, or pedimented, concealing the roof entirely. The placard so formed was used for advertising.

The pride of the town was inevitably expressed in the town hall or council chambers which, in the case of Bendigo, rivalled the equivalent in capital cities both in size and magnificence. In some towns the architectural expression is more humble and yet there is always a striving for civic expression within the architecture.

The towns which are included in this book have one aspect in common, they have architectural and planning unity. Invariably they were built during the last century when issues such as civic pride and dignity were important.

At the turn of the century few new country towns were planned. Sir John Sulman in New South Wales put forward a new concept for town planning which in a letter to Sir Henry Parkes, Premier of New South Wales, says:

. . . this mode I have distinguished as the spider's web plan in contradiction to the rectangular mode at present in vogue. It is not of course universally applicable but offers a basis to work upon which would, I think, prove far more useful than that ordinarily adopted.

Little heed was paid to the planners at this stage. The tradition of planning development of Australia lay with the surveyors or the engineers and not the architects and artists. Walter Burley Griffin was an exception. He was a Chicago architect steeped in the tradition of the 'organic' philosophies of the 'Chicago School' consisting of Louis Sullivan and Frank Lloyd Wright. He was awarded the commission for the plan of the National Capital in Canberra, after a world-wide competition in 1911. The plan was based upon two axes, a water axis created by flooding the river basin and creating a series of lakes, and a land axis between two hills, Mt Ainslie and Capitol Hill. On the land axis the buildings of state were to be erected.

The plan is essentially organic in its development of road networks clinging to the contours which gave emphasis to the land form. This gives the motorist and pedestrian a feeling for the very contour itself. Provisions were also made for a commercial centre to be divorced from the administrative core.

This was Griffin's major work, but he was also responsible for the town plans of Leeton and Griffith in New South Wales where the same axial approach to planning principles applies with the flamboyance of concentric whirls generating residential development.

Since Griffin little has been done on a grand scale. The recent mining towns created in Queensland and Western Australia have little of the vigour of the towns which were built during the mining boom of the 1850s. They are studied, controlled, conforming to preconceptions in planning and neglect the great tradition of urban form which was created in the past, even though it was created within the strictest discipline of a gridiron structure. Builders, architects and clients may have been better mannered in civic terms in former times and therefore able to create a consistency of street architecture and yet preserve diversity of detail within the single architectural unit.

Architecture today should give the necessary flexibility of self expression, but it does not. Technology has allowed the imagination of the architect and builder to be translated directly into building without many constraints. The result of this is that every architectural unit within the town can be 'self expressed'. Each unit vies for attention and the result is disastrous. No longer is there a unifying element such as a verandah which was able to continue a simple rhythm and theme throughout the town, tying together discordant pieces of architectural display. Today we have the cantilevered awning which is visually boring. Even the flexibility, colour, texture and variety created by canvas awnings along the footpath would be a better solution for shade and protection as this would afford the necessary variety of form and colour which these towns now lack.

Planners throughout the world have spoken of regional significance, national identity. Regions have been defined as organic identities, an interrelated section of a country, a natural unit which can contain its own economy and self reliance and, through this, develop a cultural pattern which is distinctive. It is generally agreed that regional cultural expression is almost extinct and the only hope in the future lies in national expression. It would be boring to contemplate a world where every city and every town bore the same stylistic influences, philosophies and appearances, despite country or climate, and yet this situation appears to be happening. Art, architecture and planning are now in the international melting pot, especially in Australia, and only a small fraction of our community participating in the visual arts is unashamedly Australian. Let us have our verandahed broad walks which are functionally necessary. Let us keep the few towns which still express our past and our heritage. Such precincts express a way of life which may have past, but the urban expression and architectural form is still valid for twentieth century living.

Ross

Tasmania

Aerial view of Ross. Note the consistent subdivision of land into paddocks some of which are surrounded by hedges in the English manner.

Right
A view from Ross Bridge across an Arcadian landscape.

Governor Macquarie with his cavalcade consisting of a military attachment and a surveyor visited Tasmania in 1811 and passed through the area around the present site of Ross.

Macquarie was impressed by the country he had examined on this tour and in 1812 instructed Surveyor Meehan and his deputy Mr Evans 'to commence their surveys . . . they will proceed overland to the Derwent and mark out the road for travellers.' Meehan was also instructed 'to travel by the same route across the country to Hobart Town by which you accompanied me in December last . . . chaining the whole of the distance between the two settlements and making such remarks as may occur to you during the journey respecting . . . the soil, timber, rivers, creeks or ponds . . . not forgetting to erect on strong posts or trees the finger-boards containing the names . . . of the several plains, rivers, mountains etc. . . . in conspicuous places.' Settlers and the military followed this early route and selected land for farming and grazing. This influx of people resulted in a military post being established at Ross in 1812, to protect travellers and pioneers from the attacks of Aboriginals and bushrangers.

Macquarie returned to Tasmania in 1821 and arrived at the site of Ross on 1 June where he found a small settlement. The 'Stocker's Inn', later called 'Man O'Ross Hotel', had been built on the west bank of the river. The next day Macquarie wrote 'I named our last night's station Ross, in honour of H. M. Buchanan Esquire, that being the name of his seat on Loch Lomond in Scotland . . .'

The earliest location orders in Ross were in favour of Charles and Henrietta Bowen and these were granted by Sir Thomas Brisbane, Governor of New South Wales, on 30 June 1823. These grants give their location as being in the Division of Lennox, originally portion of the present County of Somerset. Grants were subsequently made to Thomas Midwood 2,000 acres, Samuel Horton 1,000 acres, Benjamin Horne 4,000 acres, W. Kermode 2,000 and 1,000 acres, G. C. Clark 2,000 acres, Geo. Scott 500 acres and John Leake 2,000 acres.

By 1821 cattle were being run on Crown land at Ross for use as working bullocks and to supply persons holding government positions with milch cows. A bridge was also commenced at this time. The *Hobart Town Gazette* of 2 March 1822 reported '. . . that this very useful work has fourteen arches, and will obviate the inconvenience, hitherto felt by the overflowing of that stream in the next season by securing a safe and good passage at all times.' The bridge had a wooden superstructure resting on stone piers with a causeway at one end and was built under the supervision of Major Bell.

Detail of the voussoirs on Ross Bridge, probably the work of convict masons Daniel Herbert and James Colbeck, who were especially employed for their excellent craft ability.

Right
The original bridge at Ross was a timber structure but due to faulty foundations had to be replaced. The present bridge was designed by John Lee Archer. Work commenced in 1832 and the bridge was completed in 1836.

The hopes that the *Gazette* had expressed were not fulfilled for the major supporting piers had been built on a mud foundation and were constantly under repair. In March 1831 Roderic O'Connor, the Inspector of Roads, recommended that the bridge be superseded by a new structure, and in the following year the Colonial Engineer, John Lee Archer, inspected the site. He designed the local freestone bridge which exists today. The work is a marvel of craftsmanship and is one of the most noble bridges in the Commonwealth.

Work began slowly on the bridge. Differences of opinion arose between the fiery Roderic O'Connor and Archer as to the location. However, Archer won and the bridge was built on his recommendation. No competent masons were employed at first, until Archer recommended that Daniel Herbert and James Colbeck, two convict masons, be sent to Ross as overseers. They were paid 1s. a day and had the promise of a conditional pardon when the bridge was completed. Their conduct proved satisfactory and it is probable that these two men were responsible for the bridge's intricate carvings. In 1836 it was completed and the old bridge blown up as soon as the opening ceremony was performed. The bridge is in excellent condition and the stone work has weathered to a dark brown patina.

A gentleman called Widowson travelled to Ross in 1829 and described:
After passing "Man O'Ross" a small inn for travellers, you cross the Macquarie over a bridge between two and three hundred feet in length . . . This spot has been selected as the site most suitable for a township and as regards a fine dry soil, plenty of water, with an open, well populated country, it is perhaps a very desirable situation . . . There are also some good freestone quarries close to the township.

The town of Ross continued to grow at a steady pace under the protection of the military. Their crest can be seen in the doorway of the present library, originally the military headquarters of the district. Public houses and inns were constructed to cope with the passing trade. The 'Man O'Ross', built in 1817, became the 'Ross Hotel' in 1830 when the new part of the present hotel was erected. It is the only licensed hotel existing in the town today. Other inns were the 'Sherwood Castle' 1832; 'The Scotch Thistle' now 'Chew Magna', a private house; the 'White Conduit House' and the 'Victoria Hotel'.

The spiritual life of the town was cared for when the foundation stone of St John's Church of England was laid in 1835. However, no building took place until 1848. In 1868 the church was rebuilt and R. Kermode of 'Mona Vale' bore most of the cost. The first Methodist church was built in 1839, replaced in 1885 by the present chapel. The Wesleyan Church established

The façade of the old military headquarters, now the Library.

Right
One of the most pleasant aspects of Ross is the generous tree-lined main street where the principal buildings are situated. The town has the informality of an English village created by the grass verges to the roads which soften the streetscape. The town has a consistent quality of building due to use of stone. Although buildings in this town belong to different periods, they have the same unity as the best village architecture in England.

one of the first and most famous education centres in Australia at Ross, Horton College, named after Captain Samuel Horton. In 1850 Horton offered the Wesleyan Church twenty acres of 'Sommercotes' and £1,350 to establish a boys' school.

The foundation stone, according to the newspaper report, was laid at noon on 6 January 1852. After many and varied presidents, William Fox accepted the position as headmaster, arriving from England in 1863 to take up his post. The buildings were added to in the same year and the school consisted of a central block, a north wing and a south wing. Just when the school seemed set for a long term of usefulness and service to the community Mr Fox retired because of ill health and, shortly after, the Great Depression struck Australia. 1892 found the school in a hopeless financial state and the trustees decided to close it and hand the property back to the Horton estate. At the end of World War I the school was demolished and the homestead 'Horton' constructed from some of the materials.

In 1862 a petition was signed by fifty residents of Ross to have the district proclaimed a municipality. Following the petition, a proclamation was published on 30 December 1862 in the *Gazette*.

Ross has a Georgian quality all of its own—the main street is straight and graced with neat Georgian buildings built from the excellent freestone which takes on a golden hue in the afternoon light.

There are no surprises of a spatial nature within the town, no alleys or lanes which hold special interest or mystery. The town is as obvious as its straight street system indicates. The main street comes to its climax with the war memorials and church. At right angles to this street is the real excitement of the village, the Ross Bridge, which leads the eye across the broad landscape. Viewed from any angle, the structure is magnificent. This bridge is a romantic element in the landscape, its sensitively-proportioned arches and superbly carved voussoirs give interest at close range as well as from a distance. It is possible to descend stone steps beside the bridge and walk to a vantage point to ponder this structure. Under the bridge the Macquarie River moves swiftly while fishermen cast their rods. This is Izaak Walton country and, beyond the bridge, the village of Ross nestles amongst trees.

The 'Scotch Thistle Hotel', is the oldest hotel surviving in Ross.

Right
The successful integration between the built form and nature, so easily lost in townscapes, can be appreciated in Ross. Both built form and nature form a unity.

Over left
One of the most beautiful approaches to the bridge is from Ross itself, along a tree-lined road protected by bollards and chains. These form a gentle rhythm which anticipates the architecture of the bridge.

Over right
The first Roman Catholic priests to visit Ross generally stayed at the Military Barracks and conducted services principally for the troops. The present church was originally an old store whose walls were raised and the roof and tower added.

Oatlands

Tasmania

Aerial view of Oatlands.

Right
The Oatlands Mill, first known as the Carrington Mill, was constructed in 1837 by John Vincent. When the mill was in use it was operated by both steam and wind and drove two pairs of stones in addition to other necessary machinery.

Lachlan Macquarie named and selected the town of Oatlands in June 1821. In July of that same year he wrote to Sorell:

I strongly recommend that every reasonable encouragement should forthwith be given to such useful Mechanics as feel disposed to settle and take their Lands at the four Townships, I have pointed out the sites of . . . namely, Perth, Campbelltown, Oatlands and Brighton . . .

In September 1826 the Land Commissioners, Roderic O'Connor and Peter Murdoch, were sent to the Oatlands district to determine the exact location of the town. They chose the site beside the 'Great Lagoon', now known as Lake Dulverton.

On 31 May 1827 O'Connor and Murdoch reported that the Staff Corps were employed building a barrack. A dam had also been built to improve the lake depth and to ensure a plentiful supply of water in case of drought.

William Sharland—instructed by the Acting Surveyor-General, General Dumaresq—laid out the town in 1827. In his report on Oatlands he noted:

. . . the Land North of the town is low and marshy, and not calculated for Building upon, it will notwithstanding be very desirable and a great acquisition to the Town, the Land being very good I beg to recommend its being given away in moderate sized allotments from 3 to 10 acres to persons who may choose to build upon the Township and who may find it to their advantage to drain it.

The town started at the northern end of Lake Dulverton. Streets were marked out, trees and the scrub cleared. A detachment of troops was sent from Hobart Town to guard the farmers and the tradespeople from possible attacks from the natives and bushrangers. The detachment was under the command of Lieutenant Wilford, and the first camp was near the present flour mill along the banks of the lake.

By the following March (1828), a good deal of the clearing had been completed, and some buildings were nearing completion. Consequently the Royal Staff Corps detachment was withdrawn and finally disbanded.

The predominant building material in Oatlands was stone, obtainable along the Lake's edge. Steps along the banks can still be seen where the stone was quarried.

The town progressed with such customary buildings as officers' quarters, gaol, inns and churches. The Old Court House is the oldest building in Oatlands and was erected in 1829 as a combined chapel and police office. Thomas Anstey, the Police Magistrate, wrote in 1829:

I think the size of the Building is 32 feet by 20 feet, it is constructed of solid Masonry and Shingled—

and I believe it will be found to be the cheapest work of the kind ever performed by Government—it having been erected and covered in by two men wearing their Irons the whole time . . .

The first gaol in Oatlands was built in 1827 from timber but by 1832 John Lee Archer, the architect, reported that several of the logs were 'much decayed at the bottom'. Archer thought the buildings scarcely worth repairing, and plans were drawn up for the new gaol. By 1835 the work on the new building had commenced. The gaol accommodated the convicts working on the road and gangs employed upon government buildings.

It is interesting to read the site report for this work.

New Gaol—excavated foundation for partition walls of the four yards putting in foundations of Gaoler's House and Cross Walls of yards in rubble stone work. Building foundations of cells and room for men on route. Erecting room for do in double faced ashlar.

Do.

Do gaol walls and cells in progress for females.

Quantities of Work Performed—foundations of Rubble Stone 273 perches Walling of Gaol room for men on route and Gaoler's House, Ashlars and through 418 perches. Rough picked and draft work to the above 10,000 feet. Well in the Centre of Gaol Yard sunk 60 feet.

Quarry Road—made a new road from main quarry to the New Gaol by which a saving of cartage has accrued to Government of nearly one Mile, thereby enabling one cart to perform as much work as hitherto had employed two.

Opened a New Quarry for Ashlar approximately still nearer to the works distance about 500 yards.

The work was superintended by John Pain with Captain John Peddie as officer in charge. The building remains very much as it did in 1836.

The early roads from Oatlands were difficult to construct, especially the large stone cuttings at Spring Hill and St Peter's Pass which involved a considerable number of convicts.

The present skyline of Oatlands from the north is dominated by the tapered cylindrical shaft of the Oatlands Mill. It was first known as the Callington Mill, and built by John Vincent in 1836. It was operating as a flour mill by 1837. In 1839 Vincent tried to sell or let the mill without success and on 25 July of the next year conveyed the premises and land to his son John Jubilee Vincent. From then on the mill had various owners.

The old mill is now without its sails and structure, and the ruins of the cottages and workrooms surround it. In the *Mercury* of 17 January 1862 the mill is described as:

One of the old hotels in Oatlands. Unfortunately this building has an Art Nouveau verandah replacing an earlier one; however, the Georgian symmetry and detailing can be detected in the façade, especially in the articulated quoins. The Midlands Highway passes through the centre of town.

Once this simple Georgian expression was an hotel, the 'Midlands Hotel'.

Right
There are few stores left in Australia which contain original Georgian fittings. Note the intricately carved glazing bars to the shop window, the boarded ceiling and the cedar shelving at the rear of the store.

. . . *consisting of a two-storey built Flour Mill, with steam and wind power for driving two pairs of stones, dressing and smut machines, hoisting gear, and every necessary convenience on the most approved principal; two roomed cottage for the residence of the miller, with large stone oven, three-stall stable, dwelling house, baker's shop and two cottages, fronting on the main street, with stable and coach house adjoining; a large and well-arranged dwelling house of 12 well proportioned rooms, four stall stable with hay loft, cow shed, piggeries, yard.*

In 1881 the steam mill was fitted with a fourteen horsepower engine which was capable of turning out five to seven tons of flour daily.

The mill is now owned by the Scenery Preservation Board who intend restoring it.

There is mystery about these buildings now, and a strange eeriness has descended, perhaps due to their present derelict nature. One of the outbuildings still has its timber shingle roof defying the ravages of time.

There is unity in the architecture of Oatlands, a consistency of Georgian buildings which is rare even in Tasmania. Trucks rumble through the town but essentially it is a quiet rural village.

Much of the building in Oatlands relies on the simple balance of void and solid; its architecture is a rhythm of fenestration patterns. In most cases the buildings are simple rectangular shapes with simple pitched or gabled roofs with interest given to roofscape by chimneys. Façades are accented by doorways which are sometimes emphasised by delicately carved fanlights. Such a building was the 'Oatlands Hotel', built by Samuel Page about 1839 and run by him until his death in 1878. A notice appeared in the *Mercury* on 23 December 1880:

TO LET
THE OATLANDS HOTEL, OATLANDS:
*With the premises adjoining, comprising
large brewery, malt kiln and other
appliances, stabling for 30 horses, sale
yards, garden, etc. etc.
For term and other particulars apply to:*
Mrs. S. Page
30 Macquarie Street,
HOBART TOWN.

One of the most satisfying elements in the plan and building form at Oatlands is the long passages between buildings where glimpses of the country landscape can be viewed. Here a vista of the Church successfully terminates one of these spaces.

From this hotel Samuel Page ran coaches to Hobart Town. In Macphail's *National Directory of Tasmania 1867–68*, this stage coach run was advertised.

HOBART TOWN TO LAUNCESTON
AND VICE VERSA, BY—
Page's Day and Night Mail Coaches
Fares, Inside £2/–/–; outside £1/10/–, and
in proportion to the Intermediate Stations.
Fourteen pounds weight of Luggage allowed
each Passenger, and any excess to be charged
per lb., and in proportion to the Intermediate
Stations. Night coaches start from the Club
Hotel, Murray Street, Hobart Town, every night
(Saturdays excepted) at 20 minutes past 6 pm;
and from the Club Hotel, Brisbane Street, Launceston at
10 minutes to 6 pm; (Saturdays excepted).
Day coach leaves Hobart on Monday,
Wednesday and Friday morning and
Launceston on Tuesday Thursday and
Saturdays at 5 am.

The importance of Oatlands is its consistency of architecture and building type and the survival of many of the Georgian interiors. The grocers' shops in Oatlands have their original interiors with battened ceiling and boarded floors. In one case the shop front is beautifully designed in glazing bars with intricately patterned glazed panels. Inside the shop the scent of hams and soap, biscuits and straw brooms all combine to exude an intoxicating scent unknown in the modern supermarket.

There are few contemporary intrusions within the town. One of the most prominent (although hardly contemporary) is the Oatlands Town Hall, designed by William Lord of Hobart. A contract was let in 1880 and the hall was constructed at a cost of £1,400. The building is rather dour and has a symmetrical plan and façade. The façade has the interest of a coupled window over the main entry which gives relief to the whole.

Perched on the ridge, Oatlands could be only associated with Tasmania where a softness of light shows Georgian architecture at its best. Here the silhouette of roofs, chimneys and towers is reminiscent of a European hill village built for defence.

There is much to look at in Oatlands, and there is certainly interest in the glimpses of the countryside seen between passage ways of the shops. To view Oatlands from the fields below the town is like seeing an English town resting along the ridge with its skyline of chimney pots and gable and hip roofs, and yet all this is unified by the strong, simple quality of Georgian taste and good common sense.

Evandale

Tasmania

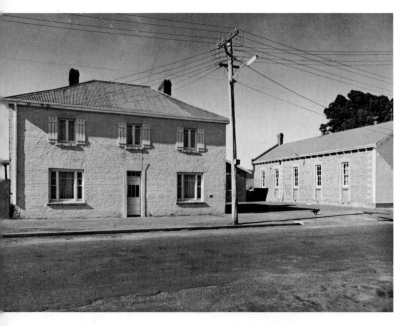

The juxtaposition of these two buildings forms an interesting urban space within the town. The two-storied building was once the 'Royal Oak Hotel,' built in 1840.

Right
The corner of High Street and Russell Street creates the centre of the town. The scale of Evandale is small and consists, for the most part, of single-storied Georgian shops and houses.

John Sinclair had worries as he stood on his verandah at 'Clairville', his new home, looking out over his fields towards Ben Lomond, with Batman's home nestling at its foot. It was late in 1834 and he had just had a deputation from local farmers seeking police protection from the emancipists—smallholders who indulged in sheep stealing, illicit distilling and sly grog selling.

In case it should be thought that this was an entirely lawless community, or perhaps because of it, in 1835 sixty-six of the leading citizens petitioned the Governor to appoint a clergyman to the district. There were already 1200 inhabitants of the district of Morven, as Evandale was then called, and in 1838 Sir John Franklin came to lay the foundation stone of the first church, which also served as a schoolroom. It stood until 1907 and was the venue for the first Evandale Show in 1868. In 1841 a new and larger Anglican church was opened but, because of faulty foundations, was demolished in 1869. The present church was designed by Henry Conway and opened in 1873.

Quite the finest building at Evandale is St Andrew's Presbyterian Church, completed in 1840, largely through the labour and enthusiasm of the Reverend Robert Russell, who had it built by day labour, supervising the work himself. Numerous Scottish settlers in the district gave him staunch support and their descendants still maintain it. The porch is supported by stalwart freestone pillars brought by special bullock waggons from Deddington, some miles away. A statue of 'Hope' is in memory of Robert Russell, who also erected the chapel at Deddington with the support of the noted artist, John Glover, who lived nearby.

In 1811 Governor Macquarie paid the first recorded visit to the district, though for four years numerous hunting parties had explored all the open country. Macquarie camped on Honeysuckle Bank, which is now Evandale, after fording the South Esk River some miles to the south, accompanied by a number of officials and his lady, all on horseback.

He came again in 1821 and made a hazardous crossing of the South Esk in flood. He and Mrs Macquarie stayed at 'Pleasant Banks' with David Gibson, who later built the fine house that still stands there.

The site of the town was first known as Collins' Hill, after George Collins, son of David Collins, who came from Norfolk Island. Collins' house still stands as does that of Kennedy Murray, another from Norfolk Island, who became the first district constable in 1835. A few miles away James Cox was erecting his fine house at Clarendon in 1836. It is regarded as one

of the finest mansions in Australia and is set among English trees on the banks of the South Esk. Close by are substantial barns and stables also in the Georgian style. 'Clarendon' is now owned by the National Trust and is a Mecca for visitors. One mile east 'Strathmore' stands beside a beautiful lake, with a water mill among the trees. 'Sunnyside', across the lake, and 'Strathmore' belonged to Samuel Bryan, son-in-law to Thomas Henty.

An ambitious scheme to supply water to Launceston was the reason for Evandale's establishment. It had at first been planned two miles distant. A convict station was established and a tunnel commenced through the hill, to emerge as a fluming below Captain Barclay's house, 'Camboc'. The tunnel was never free of water and cave-ins killed several of the prisoners working in it. Wells were sunk to give access and provide ventilation, but pneumonia carried off many of the workmen and the project was abandoned.

'Clarendon' had been noted for the breeding of thoroughbreds and Merino sheep, which were also kept at 'Strathmore' for Thomas Henty. The most notable stud of Saxon sheep today is at 'Pleasant Banks', the home of R. J. L. Foster. Devon cattle were a feature of the district for over a century, though latterly Aberdeen Angus and Polled Herefords have taken their place. Racing stock is still bred here and the Evandale Agricultural Show, founded in 1868, has always been renowned for its trial of hunters. The show pavilion, which dates from 1869, has been added to several times.

Evandale has been a centre of agricultural and pastoral activity since 1820 when grazing licences and location orders were replaced by firmer titles to the land. The area consists of the central plain of the South Esk Valley and tributaries, skirted by the foothills and mountains of the Ben Lomond Range.

Evandale is the most important selling centre in the north for store cattle and sheep. The town is also a centre for transport, having the State's busiest airport, the principal railway junction and marshalling yards, and is the hub of the State highway system.

The district became a municipality in 1865, having previously been governed by a police magistrate, Robert Wales. The town was named after G. W. Evans, Surveyor, who discovered the Bathurst Plains in New South Wales.

Among the buildings of the town to have survived since 1850 may be noted the Manse, built by Reverend Russell in 1835; 'Blenheim' built as an inn in 1832; 'The Laurels' built by John Williatt about 1840; St Andrew's Presbyterian Church; the corner store opposite the

Detail of a Georgian shop front complete with engaged flute pilasters and Georgian window glazing.

Russell Street, Evandale.

Right
Russell Street, Evandale. On the left is the 'Royal Oak Hotel' and on the right Brown's Store.

Over left
The interior of St Andrew's Presbyterian Church is simple and is divided by a gallery, added at a later date. The candelabra was brought from Edinburgh and forms a rich contrast to the simple architectural space.

Over right
St Andrew's Presbyterian Church, built in 1840. The first parson was the Reverend Robert Russell whose memorial can be seen in front of the kirk. Noted pioneers of the Evandale district are buried in the church yard. This church is one of the first pieces of ecclesiastical architecture within an Australian country town.

Post Office, dating from 1840, and the store facing Russell Street which has recently been opened as a museum called the 'Horseless Carriage'. This building included a bakery and once belonged to the Clarendon estate.

Of the eight hotels which once graced the town, only the 'Prince of Wales' and the 'Clarendon' still retain their licences. The 'Royal Oak' is a private house and the rest are demolished. The original store, half-way along Russell Street, was built by Joseph Solomon in 1836, with an equally large building behind.

The R.S.L. Club was originally the first Methodist Chapel, built in 1836. 'Briar Lane Cottage' is said to have been given by George Collins to his daughter as a wedding present. 'Fallgrove' was first the home of Kennedy Murray and later of Thomas Fall. There is an old police residence opposite Morven Park.

Like many country towns in Australia, Evandale shows little change from its appearance at the turn of the century. Modern homes have been built, but they harmonise in size and appearance with what was there before. There is an increasing awareness by residents of their heritage and a pride in perpetuating it.

Richmond

Tasmania

Aerial view of Richmond.

Right
This series of Georgian cottages
illustrates the ease with which early
builders solved the design problem of a
sloping site whilst still preserving symmetrical
massing within the individual unit of
architecture. These buildings form an
excellent townscape approach.
The middle cottage was once the
'Star and Garter Hotel'.

Coal River was the name originally given to the Richmond District, so named because coal had been discovered along the river banks. Land was gradually granted to officials and settlers and in June 1814 Lieutenant-Governor Davey issued a proclamation concerning the very marked hostilities evidenced by the natives of the Coal River.

Lieutenant-Governor William Sorell was first to take steps to form a town. The Journals of the Land Commissioners for Van Diemen's Land 1826–28 tell us how land for a township was obtained. Sorell disposed of his land at Richmond to John Hunt Butcher and Dr John Barnes. In settlement of a debt of about £100, Mr Butcher sold 100 acres to Mr David Lord who, it appears, was aware that this would be required for the proposed township. Shortly after he exchanged with the Government ninety acres (the site of Richmond) for 1,400 acres in the York Plains district.

In 1832, James Backhouse, the Quaker, wrote that Richmond consisted of a Court House, a Gaol, a windmill and about thirty dwellings, three of which were inns. He visited Richmond again in February 1834, remarking that 'Richmond is nearly doubled in size'.

The early buildings mentioned by Backhouse form the nucleus of the town. The Court House, which represented law and order to the early community, was built in 1825–26, probably to the design of architect David Lambe. It was used as both church and court. Backhouse tells how the Court House was used for divine service by both Episcopalians and Wesleyans. The building is still used as a council chamber with the original furniture still in place. East of the Court House were the police buildings: the Watch House, Police Office and Constables Barracks.

Another necessary feature of early Tasmanian towns was a gaol. Richmond's was built with stone walls and covered by a shingle roof.

The northern section of the Gaol was built in 1825. John Lee Archer, the Colonial Architect, designed the internal square of the gaol created by adding cell blocks and the kitchen wing. The courtyard was completed by adding the Governor's residence in 1832. The square contains a well and was used in former times as an exercise yard.

Richmond has little form as a town, it is more a collection of buildings. However, it is unique in that the majority of the buildings were constructed in the Georgian style. The town rambles about within a more or less gridiron pattern, occasionally taking some recognition of the hilly domain on which it stands distorting the gridiron pattern.

'Oak Lodge' was built by Henry Buscombe and is one of the many fine Georgian buildings in Richmond. The architecture is a direct interpretation of an English country house without any modification for the Australian climate. Such buildings formed models for the Australian vernacular.

Right
Detail of doorway of 'Oak Lodge', Bridge Street. The delicate tracery of the fanlight and the engaged columns surrounding the doorway are worthy of attention.

The approach to Richmond from the east is across the multi-spanned stone bridge, the oldest of its type, by ten years, in Australia. The necessity for a bridge was pointed out by John Thomas Bigge, the Royal Commissioner, when he visited Van Diemen's Land in 1820. Through his efforts, Bigge's Bridge was constructed. It was built by convict labour, probably under the superintendence of Major Bell of the 48th Regiment, who was Engineer-in-Charge of Public Works, and William Wilson who was Superintendent of Stonemasons at that time. David Lambe, Second Colonial Architect, also visited the site before it was completed and may have had a hand at detailing the terminal bollards and balustrade.

Richmond became an important thoroughfare when the bridge was completed. It enabled heavy traffic to proceed to the east coast and Tasman Peninsula without delay when the Coal River was in flood, a frequent occurrence. There is a robustness about this bridge, a vigour of design which suggests a structural expediency rather than the refined treatment of Archer's elegant bridge at Ross. Nevertheless what it loses in refinement it gains in form and silhouette, and robustness of expression.

St Luke's stands on the edge of town and is one of the finest churches designed by John Lee Archer. The foundation stone was laid on 3 February 1834 by Governor Arthur and the church was entirely built by prisoners of the Crown with stone quarried from nearby Butcher's Hill. The church is elementary in design with the square tower terminating a rectangular nave. The workmanship of the church is excellent, particularly the ceiling which is a mass of trusses and strutting forming almost a web of constructional technique. The convict responsible was given his pardon for its execution. The old clock from St David's Church, Hobart Town, was installed in the tower in 1922.

The Roman Catholic Church of St John was built on the opposing hill, across the river, and is the oldest Roman Catholic Church in Australia. The land upon which St John's stands was given by John Cassidy, a parishioner, in 1810. Bishop Polding, on his way to Sydney in 1835, visited Richmond. He left the Reverend James Cotham with instructions to give Richmond special attention. It is thought that the Bishop brought plans of small churches with him, and it is possible that he blessed the foundation stone during his visit. A stone on the chancel wall bears the date 1836. The church is in strong contrast to St Luke's. St John's is Gothic-inspired with pointed arches and a spire covered with slate accented by dormer ventilators breaking the simple form.

Richmond Gaol is now a National monument. The northern end of the courtyard and the two side wings were designed by John Lee Archer.

Right
The Gaoler's residence.

St Luke's Church of England, designed by John Lee Archer, was built between 1834 and 1836. The clock was installed in 1922 from St David's, Hobart Town, after that church was demolished. The church is simple, dignified in its proportions and terminates the vista framed by trees within the town.

Right
The interior of St Luke's. Local legend says that the convict responsible for the execution of this fine ceiling was given his pardon. The expressed structure is one of the finest in Tasmania.

In 1859, the *Hobart Town Mercury* stated that St John's was considerably enlarged and decorated. The renovations and additions were designed by Frederick Thomas, an architect of some reputation, in the Gothic manner.

There are many buildings of romance and history in Richmond, in particular the old mill in East Street which was converted to a residence by the artist John Eldershaw. The mill was built in 1855 and is the only survivor of many which once graced Richmond. There are the inns such as the 'Richmond Hotel', licensee Lawrence Cotham, 1838, whose name is still visible above the tap room door. From this hotel two coaches ran between 'Mr. Master's Hotel', Hobart Town and Richmond. There is the 'Sawyer's Arms' in Gunning Street, built after 1844, which still retains the pitsawn rafters and worn manger racks in the stables.

The early towns of Australia consisted not only of inns, administration buildings, mills and churches catering for more urban living, but were essentially trading posts with general stores and granaries. The general store became the feature of all country towns. Such a general store was built in Richmond by J. K. Buscombe in 1832, and was acquired in 1897 by the Crown as a post office. The granary is still attached to the building and serves as a reminder that Richmond was known as the 'granary of Australia'.

In 1819 Andrew Bent wrote in his *Hobart Town Gazette* 'The printer of this paper begs leave to remind his Pittwater and other country subscribers that he will receive wheat from them in payment. It is hoped that those who are nearly three years in arrears with him will find it in their power to discharge the same this year.'

A picture of early Richmond is given by Thomas Scott, the surveyor, when he wrote in 1830:

. . . at 14 miles from Hobart Town the traveller enters the thriving township of Richmond. Here is a Court House, a Gaol, and Soldiers Barracks. Divine service is performed on alternate Sundays by the Rev. Mr. Garrard from Sorell. Besides several private homes, there is a good Inn kept by Mr. Buscombe. There is also an excellent flour mill originally built by Mr. John Walker and across the river is a well built stone bridge of six arches.

Boats of six tons burden came up within half a mile of this town and the tide flows as far as the bridge . . .

The natural beauty of the scenery here is much improved by the English looking mansions of Mr. Lascelles, Mr. Butcher, Major de Gillern and Mr. David Lord.

One of the English-looking mansions which Thomas Scott describes could have been

Right
The present Council Chambers, formerly the Court House. The porch, added in later years, effectively destroys the symmetry and the noble curve of the Regency Bow front. The Bow is articulated with shallow pilasters and on either side of the central court room are symmetrical pavilions. The court was built between 1825 and 1826 and probably designed by architect David Lambe.

Below
Georgian simplicity is expressed by lack of extroversion. Honesty in structure can be seen in these early buildings.

Above centre
A strangely-proportioned building is almost childlike in its composition, especially in the relation between the windows and the doors which contribute to a startled expression. The panelled shutters and the timber pilasters beside the windows are typical of the usual Georgian interpretation.

Above right
The General Store and Granary was built by J. K. Buscombe in 1832. The joinery to the shop front is excellent. Most general stores occupied a position of importance in early towns and often traded manufactured goods for crops when money was scarce.

Right
The Richmond Bridge has a ruggedness with almost an expression of structural expediency. There is no ornament and little refinement, but the whole has enormous vigour. The bridge was constructed by convict labour under William Wilson in the 1820s.

'Mayfield' which was built on part of 710 acres granted by Macquarie to William Sorell in 1819. Thomas Scott's map shows Dr John Barnes had succeeded Sorell in purchasing 'Mayfield' and David Lord purchased it about 1837. 'Oak Lodge' built by Henry Buscombe in Bridge Street, is another such English-looking mansion. The house has a magnificent doorway and fanlight and the whole of the house is merely a supplanted English country farm typical of the Georgian style quite unchanged by any climatic or geographic influences.

The character of Richmond is the English translation of the Georgian style in Australia. Whether consciously or not, the siting of major buildings is towards the picturesque and on vantage points which could encompass wide views. Certainly the placement of St John's and St Luke's illustrates this point. Richmond retains the feeling of an English village for the most, and differs in respect to the more disciplined layout expressed in the gridiron pattern of the streets influenced by the early military engineers and architects.

Berrima

New South Wales

The drinking trough outside the walls of the Gaol at Berrima.

Right
The finest building in Berrima is the Court House, designed by the Colonial Architect Mortimer Lewis. The architecture of the building is in the Regency style and consists of a central block with Doric columned portico flanked by lower wings which are slightly rusticated. The Court House, flanked by mature trees, is sited above the town and overlooks the Gaol.

In March 1818 Governor Macquarie sent James Meehan the Surveyor with Dr Charles Throsby and a party to see whether a land route could be found from Sydney to Jervis Bay.

The party progressed to the eastern section of Moss Vale on to the head of Bundanoon Creek. It was understood that here a passage would be found by which the explorers could travel to Jervis Bay. With difficulty they pressed on as far as the present site of Marulan, and here the party divided in order to test alternative routes. Throsby took the route into the Kangaroo Valley and so on to Jervis Bay. Meehan and his party went south and reached open pasture which he called Goulburn Plains, where the present town of Goulburn is situated.

For his services in the exploration of the district, Throsby was rewarded with a grant of 1,000 acres in any part of the country which he had discovered. His companions were each granted 100 acres.

Charles Throsby was born in Leicester, England, in 1771. He reached Sydney in 1802 and was appointed acting surgeon at Castle Hill, and by 1804 was sent to Newcastle where he was appointed Commandant. In 1809 he resigned through ill-health and in 1810 was granted 950 acres near Liverpool which he named 'Glenfield Park'. Exploration was obviously in Throsby's blood and he made a number of excursions into the hinterland, especially the Berrima area. Not only was Throsby actively engaged in discovery but he was responsible for the construction of the first road from Picton to the Goulburn Plains. For this service he was awarded an additional 500 acres near the original grant of 1,000 acres, which was named 'Throsby Park'.

Macquarie had been impressed by the reports of the area and in September 1819 sent a memorandum to the Commissariat Department stating:

. . . having deemed it advisable to permit Charles Throsby Esquire and Nine other Free Persons with their Families to become settlers in that part of the County of Camden recently discovered by Mr. Throsby, I have granted them Victualling Orders on the Stores at Liverpool . . .

Again Macquarie noted in his jornal his visit to the area on 19 October 1820:

. . . the situation of the New Settlers four miles south west of Throsby Park is particularly beautiful and rich— resembling a fine extensive pleasure ground in England. On seeing this sweet spot, I longed much to have Mrs. Macquarie and dear Lachlan with me to participate in the pleasure I felt on beholding so beautiful a landscape. We saw a vast number of the large forest kangaroos in this morning's excursions.

64

The detail of the Gaol gateway. Work commenced on the building in May 1834, the whole work being carried out entirely by convict labour. The building, completed in 1839, consisted of a traditional gaol plan with three wings radiating from a central watch tower. Between 1865 and 1866 considerable alterations took place and this fine gateway, as well as additional cells, was added.

Right
Berrima is one of the few surviving towns in New South Wales to retain its Georgian character. In the foreground is the former 'Commercial Inn' (now a restaurant) built by Francis Breen and later owned by D. Armfield. In the background is the former 'Crown Inn' (now an art gallery) built by William Taylor.

Surveyor-General Oxley commenced the measurement of farms in the Bargo district, north of Berrima, in 1821 and shortly after in the area south towards Berrima. On 31 March 1821 Oxley was instructed that Mr Meehan would fix a place where a town would be erected on the 'Wingee Carabie' River. This town was called Bong Bong and was some miles from the present site of Berrima. Nothing remains of the town today.

When the new road was made south, Berrima eclipsed Bong Bong completely. District magistrate James Atkinson, who had been granted land in the area, argued that Berrima was more suitable as a town site as it was closer to building material available from the limestone quarries at Marulan.

The site on which Berrima now stands appears to have been chosen in 1830 by Major Mitchell, then Surveyor-General, who was responsible for the construction of the new south road. In his report in March 1830 Mitchell suggested that the beauty of the site was such as might induce interested persons to make their homes there.

Surveyor Robert Hoddle marked out the town which included government reserves and lots for sale.

The first lot in the town was marked out for James Atkinson of 'Oldbury' in 1832. There was delay in the building of the southern road and this had the effect of delaying progress in the town itself.

Govett saw the town in 1837 and reported:

. . . a new township was laid out in 1832 . . . called Berrima. This spot is rather peculiarly situated and when I visited it for the purpose of laying out the form of the streets, the place wore a melancholy aspect. The land surrounding is barren and stony, and bushland dark and gloomy. The River Wingercarribee winds with a long and acute bend around the points fixed upon as the site of the town: through the centre the new Southern road passes. The bed and banks of the river here are rocky, and likely to afford excellent material for building. A space of ground was allotted for religious purposes on a small rounded hill . . .

Little time was lost after Govett had completed the detailed town plan. An 'iron gang' of prisoners in chains was employed on public works and a detachment of soldiers guarded the stockade in which they were kept.

Surveyor Harper was also sent to the area in 1820 to measure the early land grants, but due to illness retired and settled in Berrima, where he built his brick home in 1834 and the 'Surveyor-General Hotel' which he named after Mitchell. This inn is the oldest continually

The 'Surveyor-General Hotel' was originally constructed by Surveyor Harper who was sent to the Berrima district in 1820 to measure the early land grants. He built the hotel in 1834, and named it after Sir Thomas Mitchell. It is the oldest continually licensed inn in New South Wales. The original structure survives but the alteration to the fabric of the building, especially the fenestration details and the removal of plaster, has done much to mutilate it.

Right
Harper's house, built by William Harper, surveyor for Berrima.

licensed inn in New South Wales, but at present suffers from mutilation of the exterior by the removal of the lime plaster which once covered its irregular walls. The verandah is much altered as are the window details, and the building has generally lost the patina of age which can never be replaced.

Harper's house itself is a fine Georgian-type two-storey mansion which stands on the hill overlooking the town. The building is symmetrical about a front door with a low-slung verandah in the front, and has a symmetrical axis about an enlarged central window.

The census of 1841 recorded a population of 249 with thirty-seven houses finished and seven in the course of erection. Ten years later the population had fallen to 192 with no increase in the number of houses.

The Gaol was commenced with convict labour in 1837, but much of the original building is now concealed. The imposing entrance was constructed in sandstone in 1866, framed on either side with pilasters and curved walls and built as a studied form of gaol monumentality with massive timber doors guarding the entrance. The building originally consisted of three wings, each wing having two floors, forming six corridors with the wings radiating out from the centre. On top of the central block was a watch tower.

In the years 1865–66 eight new cells were added to each wing, the outside walls were raised another five feet and the present entrance built. To intensify the silence within the gaol all men had to wear felt shoes inside.

Notorious names of Australia are associated with the Gaol—'Thunderbolt' (Fred Ward), the Clerks, Lowrie, Gilbert, the Dunns and, of course, the romantic 'Starlight'.

The Court House adjacent to the Gaol is one of Australia's finest piece of colonial architecture. It was designed by the Colonial Architect, Mortimer Lewis, between 1810 and 1830. The building is Regency in its character and has a symmetrical composition about a central court house block. The columns are Doric and form a portico with classical pediment complete with metopes. The flanking pavilions are slightly rusticated and terminate in curved blocks. On either side of the front door to the court within the portico are niches with carved curved tops to emphasise the solidity of the wall and to give variation to the composition.

Contrary to some opinion, the entasis on the columns is wrong and has the corrective 'bulge' in the shaft too close to the base. This mistake gives the building a suitable colonial quality.

68

The Common at Berrima is now forested by pines. The low-scaled verandah building in the foreground was built as a private residence by Jerome Higgins but at one time was used as a school.

Around the town are various buildings, the most important grouping being around the Common shaded by a stand of ancient pines. There is a magnificent low-slung vernacular home originally built by Jerome Higgins, one time store keeper and Post Master. Crowning the Common is the Holy Trinity Church designed by Edmund Blacket and consecrated in 1849.

In 1838 the Roman Catholic community commenced negotiations for the purchase of the old stockade for the erection of a school, church and presbytery. Work was slow on the church, which was started in 1849 and completed in 1851. Both the Holy Trinity and St Francis Xavier churches are simple Gothic revival without particular architectural merit; however, they do sit within the townscape extremely well, especially as the colour of the ashlar sandstone walls throws a gold hue amongst the pines.

Among other buildings of merit the inn with the hipped roof, adjacent to the Gaol, is the most prominent. Today the building is a restaurant. Running at right angles to the Hume Highway is Jellore Street, which contains a row of Georgian cottages of various shapes and proportions but all having the front doors protected by low-scaled verandahs. Amongst this group is the old 'Victoria Inn' built by Joseph Levy who advertised in 1836 that 'he was now residing at Berrima where he had opened a store.'

There is much to see of the architecture of Georgian New South Wales in Berrima. It is the only Georgian town of this period, left in that State and for this reason it should be cherished. It has many qualities as a town, especially the siting of the Gaol and the Court House on high ground above the town proper, and the generous scale of the Common accentuated by low-scaled Georgian buildings surrounding it.

Of course there has been mutilation, the fibro additions, the hoardings and signs, the pollution of twentieth century living as well as the surge of traffic through the town. But Berrima copes with all these problems; it has enough breadth to absorb these activities.

There, below the town, the Wingercarribee River flows on as quietly as ever.

Carcoar

New South Wales

A view of the town of Carcoar from Naylor Street.

Right
Carcoar nestles at the bottom of a hill under the protection of a church spire. Because of the hill, the architecture has been stepped accordingly, creating diverse shapes between the juxtaposition of the buildings.

Carcoar sleeps in a small valley about nine miles south of Blayney on the Olympic Highway in New South Wales. It is the third oldest town west of the Blue Mountains, its growth taking place from 1839. The town was built on the northern bank of the Belubula River, a tributary of the Lachlan, on reasonably hilly country which flattens towards the south. The district around Carcoar was discovered from 1815 onwards when Assistant-Surveyor G. W. Evans passed through on his way to explore the western interior.

Between 1821 and 1828 there is evidence of temporary occupation of the country situated westward of Bathurst—and in 1830 George Ranken of 'Kellochiels', Bathurst, formed a station near the present town of Woodstock, between Carcoar and Cowra.

From 1828 to 1835 Assistant-Surveyor James B. Richards from Survey Headquarters at Bathurst was engaged in dividing Westmoreland, as this country was then known, into four counties which were named Bathurst, Roxburgh, Westmoreland and Georgiana, and in the course of his surveys made reservations for villages at Blackman's Swamp (Orange), Carcuan (Carcoar) and King's Plains (Blayney).

Thomas Icely took possession of a grant of 560 acres on 26 May 1829 around the present town of Carcoar. The history of Carcoar is much concerned with this man who was born at Plympton County, Devon, in 1797, the eldest son of a merchant and ship owner. In 1819 he embarked for New South Wales, bringing with him valuable commodities which he sold for great profit in Sydney, and he established a merchant's business in George Street. Icely also had a letter from Lord Bathurst to Governor Macquarie with instructions that he should receive a grant of 600 acres but, before taking this up, Icely returned to England with the object of extending the proposed grant to 2,000 acres. This was granted by Under-Secretary Goulburn and an additional 560 acres was added to the property under the 'free grant' system. The Bathurst district in 1829–30 experienced a severely dry spell and, under these circumstances, Icely built his first homestead on the left bank of the Belubula in the angle contained by that stream and its confluence with Coombing Creek, opposite the village reserve of Carcuan (now Carcoar). He named his property 'Coombing', probably after the suburb of Devonport where Icely's father resided in England.

In the same year as Icely established himself at 'Coombing', Frederick John and William Montague Rothery, obtained grants of 2,460 acres each, twelve miles west of 'Coombing' on the left bank of Limestone Creek, which they named 'Cliefden Springs' and 'Cliefden'.

The railway station at Carcoar is Gothic and can be seen from the main road. It is a romantic folly set against the hill. The building has a symmetrical composition about a central pavilion with public conveniences on either side balancing the whole.

Right
St Paul's Church of England, Carcoar, is situated on the corner of Belubula and Collins Streets and holds a commanding position over the town. It was designed by Edmund Blacket and is believed to be a replica of the parish church in Plymton, England, the home of Thomas Icely of 'Coombing Park'. The foundation stone was laid in 1845 and the tower and steeple were added in 1874–75.

Icely continued to add to 'Coombing' with purchases which consolidated it to some 13,000 acres and formed the foundation of Coombing Park. The first substantial home was 'Stoke Cottage', built by Icely for his overseer. It was a rude timber affair lined internally with lathe and plaster. Additions of brick were made and it still remains.

'Old Coombing Cottage' was built between 1838 and 1839. The present stone stables at 'Coombing' date from 1842. Around this first settlement many other buildings have been erected, forming a small village in itself. Following violence and bushranging at this isolated and primitive settlement a police barracks and depot was constructed in 1838 across the river from 'Stoke Cottage' and about half a mile from Icely's home at the junction of the Cowriga and Belubula Creeks. These buildings appear to have been the first government buildings erected in Carcoar. Nothing remains of them now, as they would have been constructed from timber and bark in accordance with practice of the day.

On 20 September 1838 the Surveyor-General instructed Assistant-Surveyor Walker Ramine Davidson to lay out the Reserve of Carcuan. In August 1839 the Government approved the plan. The first sale of town allotments took place on 6 July 1840, and these were submitted to public auction. The town consisted of eleven streets and, across the creek, Icely created his own subdivision of three streets. The streets were called after the pioneers of the district—Icely, Rothery, Ivory, Danvers, Collins, Rodd and Jones, whilst others were named after places— Mandurama, Coombing, Belubula and Goomballo. The main street, Naylor Street, which is at present part of the Olympic Highway, was named after the first Anglican minister, the Reverend Thomas Beagley Naylor.

The town of Carcoar began to grow and by March 1842 tenders were called for a court house and lock up. This building stood until 1882 when it was replaced by the present Italianate design. The Court House also served as the meeting hall and the church.

In 1846 Governor FitzRoy, newly arrived in the Colony, planned a visit to the country around Bathurst. On 17 November his cousin, Lieutenant-Colonel G. C. Mundy who accompanied the Governor together with other officials, recalled the visit to Carcoar:
Passing through the town of Bathurst, we came upon a fine undulating lightly wooded and tolerably well grassed country. The road we took was a mere bush track, but the wheels ran lightly on the glittering granite soil, and tolerably smoothly except when we fell among rocks on the area of some ridges . . . The last six miles of the new road into Carcoar had just been marked out and partially

made by the inhabitants expressly for the Governor . . . After a long and latterly steep descent through a densely wooded and hilly country, we suddenly dropped down upon the snug-looking village of Carcoar, seated on the banks of a river in a hollow vale . . . At the loyal town of Carcoar, His Excellency was received with triumphal arches, pistol shots—for I saw no advance of large calibre— cheers, agitated cabbage tree hats, and, of course an address. Our exit from the town suffered somewhat in dignity from the jaded state of our horses. His Excellency had to double thong his wheeler, and "tip the silk" to his leaders up a very steep ascent from the river . . . The Colonial Secretary and myself . . . were at one moment with the eyes of Carcoar upon us, in a state of abject fear lest our Phaeton should perform the humiliating act of retrogression.

By 1850 Carcoar was the most popular town, after Bathurst, west of the Blue Mountains. It had three coaches per week running between it and Bathurst and the population was about 500 persons which grew to 600 between 1866 and 1878.

Carcoar is a romantic town; the road turns sharply down into the town from Bathurst with the grey shingle spire of St Paul's on the left and the rectory on the right. St Paul's was designed by Edmund Blacket and constructed in brick. It was completed on 6 December 1849. A spire was added by a builder called James Shakespeare in 1874 and this gives the church an additional village quality. Other churches followed. The Roman Catholic Church was constructed in 1870 of fine stone and the Presbyterian Church and manse in 1861. By 1866 there were six hotels in Carcoar bearing names such as the 'Victoria', 'Old Royal', 'White Horse', 'Australian Arms'.

With the discovery of gold in New South Wales in 1851, prospectors began fossicking around the Carcoar area. Thomas Icely as a consequence threw open a part of Coombing Park for prospecting but this proved subsequently to be a 'duffer'. A Mr Alford of Carcoar records 200–300 Chinese to about twenty whites in ratio were prospecting in the district. There appears to have been little success with gold, although finds of copper and iron ore were made at Coombing Park.

Carcoar flourished until 1876, when the Western Railway Line was completed from Bathurst to Blayney. Although it was the intention to continue the line further, Carcoar languished for twelve years until the line caught up with the town. Carcoar was reached by catching the train to Blayney, and then coaching the rest of the way over extremely bad roads. The railway reached Carcoar by 1888, but it was all too late. Other towns had

progressed and the advent of better transport made little difference to the town.

The town has the traditional colours of dull gold and brown, the windows are shaded by verandahs and the scale of the street is low and human. At the bottom of the hill is Clarke's Enterprise Store, which was built in the 1860s. The original cedar shop fittings exist, with their dull glow reflecting the light from the cedar framed windows and the buildings basking in the sun across the street. Carcoar relies much on its picturesque grouping, especially the way it straddles the hill. Seen across the creek the town has a nobility expressed in so many English villages with the protective influence of the church spire.

The town is intact although much restoration is needed, especially in the smaller buildings which are usually the victims of mutilation. The public buildings and churches are sound, and these give the strength and dignity to the town.

Recent proposals have been put into effect to divert the Olympic Highway away from the town. By this it is hoped that the thundering traffic through Naylor Street will cease as a step in preserving Carcoar as one of New South Wales' finest towns.

Gulgong

New South Wales

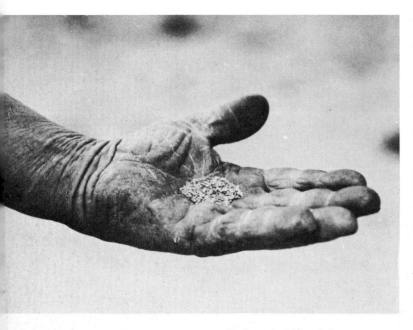

The lure of gold founded many towns in New South Wales. Here gold was photographed in an Aboriginal's hand in the 1870s. Mitchell Library Collection.

Right
A contemporary view of Gulgong which retains some of the feeling of the gold rush although most of the buildings mentioned in the text during the time of the celebrated novelist, Anthony Trollope, have gone. These were replaced in the 1870s and 1880s with more permanent structures which make up Gulgong today.

Of the many gold towns in Australia Gulgong is one of the best preserved and the most picturesque. It is not typical of the Australian town plan which was formally established on a gridiron pattern.

In Australia the main street is the most dominant element and it is here the main commercial activity is conducted. The side streets are almost insignificant by comparison, as if they were mere alleys. Gulgong has a slightly curving main street where the urbanscape is filled with the excitement of change and expectation of new urban composition.

There is an added quality to Gulgong for little has changed over the years. The buildings still have their verandahs intact and appear to be in reasonable repair, the pubs have original hoardings and signs, and there is an air of nineteenth century pride within the town, marred only by some recent rebuilding of a bank in a mediocre expression of twentieth century architecture.

Lieutenant William Lawson explored the area north from Bathurst in search of the Liverpool Plains during November 1820, and again in 1821. He passed beyond the present position of the town of Mudgee and travelled down the Gudgegong River. He left that stream and journeyed northwards across the hills to the junction of the Eurunderee (Pipe Clay) Creek and the Splash Back Creek and from here moved northward again to the Talbragar River before returning to Bathurst.

His reports on the country were impressive and this stimulated the interests of George and Henry Cox, sons of William Cox, into taking up land in that district. It was agreed between the two families that the Lawsons would apply for grants on the north of the Gudgegong River and the Cox brothers on the south.

In 1823 Allan Cunningham returned from his first exploratory trip to the Liverpool Plains and traversed the Gulgong district from the opposite direction taken by Lawson. Cunningham's records indicate that Lawson was possibly the first white man in the Gulgong district.

Following the decisions of Lawson and Cox to settle on the Gudgegong, other people quickly followed and soon there were many holdings along the river. The first lands legally occupied in the Gulgong district were granted as early as 1825 by Governor Brisbane, for services rendered, to Mr Richard Rouse who came to Australia in 1801 as Governor of Works in New South Wales on behalf of the Imperial Government. On his retirement from

Right & over

These are selected photographs from the Holtermann Collection of photographs on Gulgong in the Mitchell Library Collection. In the reminiscences of G. C. Johnson: 'Gulgong had three distinct stages. It was at first mean and sordid. Even stringy bark was not in evidence as a building material . . . It was the ugliest town I ever saw, though it was not for long, for the era of Dubbo pine and stringy bark set in, and with them a better class of building. The streets of Gulgong in the early days were weird and wonderful both in shape and make . . . The main street was long and sinuous, with a falling gradient all the way down to Adams lead and the Guntawong Road. It might have been picturesque but it was abominably mean looking . . . Gulgong was without doubt the most crowded thoroughfare in Australia. It was a blaze of lights at night . . . the pubs were doing a roaring trade, so were the shanties.'

this position Rouse took up more land known as Guntawang and Biraganbi. It was about this time that the name Gulgong appeared on the first map of the Colony prepared by Thomas Mitchell, but the reason for its inclusion is not known and apparently referred to the district only.

Between 1842 and 1872 the Rouse holdings were expanded until the property totalled 1,956 acres or sixty per cent of the alienated land. It was during this time that reports of the first gold discoveries were made.

One of them was made in October 1852 by Mr S. Stutchbury, who discovered a conglomerate near Gulgong which contained gold. In 1859 further finds were reported at Guntawang and at Green Swamp about ten miles south of Gulgong. A newspaper article 'Golden Gulgong' states:

. . . *it was in 1870 that gold was first found on what is known as Red Hill, a few hundred yards from the post office. From the year of the first discovery until 1876 over thirty-two tons of gold were won, and during that time the name of Gulgong was known in every corner of the earth. The gold was literally picked up off the surface of the ground, and even to this day children find it a profitable pastime to go "specking" after rain on Red Hill and about the thousands of abondoned shafts which surround the town.*

Shortly before the end of 1870 there were 800 persons on the field and, following the discoveries of Adams Lead, the population swelled to 3,000. Further discoveries in rapid succession, known as Happy Valley, Caledonian and Canadian, followed in 1872 with a further discovery at Home Rule, increasing the population to over 20,000 by 1873.

The township of Gulgong was surveyed in August 1870, with reservations for the various churches and the school. It is possible to imagine the stores, pubs, and churches constructed from a variety of materials, when looking at Holtermann's photographs. For most of the miners, the digger's residence was more often a small calico tent on the slopes of his claim. There were a few log huts with chimneys constructed from various materials—clay, sticks, iron sheets—which displayed much imagination and ingenuity.

The furniture consisted of one or two stumps of trees for chairs and most probably a tea chest or box served as a table. The bed was a stretcher or bunk made of forked stakes and saplings covered with a rug and one or two blankets.

Two days' travelling took Trollope, the celebrated English author, from the gold rush town of Sofala to Gulgong, spelt Gullgong in his book, on his journeys in New South Wales and Queensland.

Gullgong was certainly a rough place when I visited it, but not quite as rough as I had expected. There was an hotel there, at which I got a bedroom to myself, though but a small one, and made only of slabs. But a gorgeously grand edifice was being built over our heads at the time. The inhabited part of the town consisted of two streets at right angles to each other, in each of which every habitation and shop had probably required but a few days for its erection. The fronts of the shops were covered with large advertisements, the names and praises of traders as is customary now with all new-fangled marts, but the place looked more like a fair than a town . . .

There were butchers and bakers, grocers and drapers, banks, hotels and wine shanties in abundance. Trollope was entertained in royal style with a civic reception being afforded him by the town dignitaries at 'Selff's Hotel', one of the first to be licensed in Gulgong. G. C. Johnson describes it as a long, low verandahed building very typical of the low-scaled buildings seen in the Holtermann photographs.

In the book which he wrote on life in the Colony, Trollope told of going down a mine 150 feet deep—an experience he did not care for—and watching alluvial dirt being brought to the surface, puddled, washed and the gold extracted. What amazed him most was that the men all looked alike clothed in flannel shirts, moleskin trousers, cloth caps or felt hats, and butcher boots, and all with their faces heavily bewhiskered.

Town life in Gulgong slowly became more sophisticated. Early in 1871 hearings for the Court of Petty Sessions were gazetted and two banks had opened their doors for business, the Australian Joint Stock Bank and the Bank of New South Wales.

Gulgong's first newspaper the *Gulgong Guardian* was sold and the winding bush track along which the first buildings were strung out was named Queen Street, later to be renamed Mayne Street.

Civic pride expressed itself in true Victorian fashion—a hospital was erected by popular subscription around this time, the Presbyterian and Methodist Churches were established and the Roman Catholic community had begun to replace their temporary weatherboard structure with stone.

By 1874 the decline of the goldfields was becoming apparent, although hopes of revival were maintained and Gulgong still prospered. This was evidenced in the Church of England community deciding to build a new church to replace 'the miserable structure' which had been in continual use. In 1876 the town was constituted under the 'Municipal District of Gulgong'.

As the mining reports worsened it was realised that the country was exhausted of its rich loads and gradually grazing activity was undertaken. In *Moore's Almanac* from 1879 onwards there is less emphasis on mining activity and more on pastoral progress. At this stage Gulgong seems to have been at its zenith, with stores and offices, pubs, the bakery and a host of small cottages built around the fringe of a bustling centre.

Flour milling was commenced by Mr C. R. Young whose name appears on the mill as early as 1844. This is now the skin stores used by Messrs Jas. Loneragan (Gulgong) Pty Ltd. The area became famous for its wheat—this is evidenced by an article in the *Gulgong Advertiser*, 7 January 1898. '. . . the area of land under wheat is greater than it has ever been and had it not been for the drought, this community would have been one of the most prosperous in New South Wales.'

Mr Young owned Gulgong's first general store and sold it in 1902 to Jas. Loneragan's Milling Company Ltd. This store is still in existence on the corner of Mayne and Herbert Streets and is one of the most important buildings, visually, in the street. Other shops followed and were incorporated into the general urban scene. In all cases wide verandahs sheltered the shop fronts and afforded shade on the hot summer days, or in winter gave shelter from the wind and rains. Each verandah was different in its detailing, depending upon the date of its erection. The current fashionable style, whether it be Gothic overtones in lace or the more robust timber lattice forms of the 1890s, was incorporated on the verandah columns and valences, and this variation in design style gave richness and diversity to the streets in Gulgong. They are living architectural history books, and passing styles can easily be detected.

To compare recent photographs of Gulgong with those of Holtermann is reassuring—much has changed and yet the change is subtle, and this gives Gulgong an importance. It enables the historian, sociologist, architect and artist an unparalleled view of what a gold rush town was like. So many of the other famous towns, such as Hill End, have virtually vanished and only a few buildings remain to signify that the town existed.

Although the centre of the town has permanent buildings of stone and brick, buildings of the gold rush days still stand. When conditions were less permanent and life depended upon the luck of the find, one was not so concerned with the architectural qualities of a house. Little houses were constructed from mud brick or pisé—vernacular houses with central

The Holtermann photographs give extraordinary insight into the life style of Gulgong during the gold rush era. Each photograph tells its own story and there is little need for interpretation.

doorway and symmetrically placed windows, a small chimney and originally a timber shingle roof. Some can still be seen in the back streets of Gulgong. They are simply scaled and low, the eaves of the verandah sometimes are only 5′ 6″ in height and they are often further reduced by creepers. Some stand proudly in the street with picket fences or shrubberies defining the small property boundaries, and occasionally there are examples of split rail fences surrounding the rear orchard or vegetable patch.

The opening of the railway represented the most important event in later years. This occurred on the 14 April 1909, the anniversary of the discovery of gold. With the coming of the railway, Gulgong became a flour-milling centre. This change to an agricultural economy ensured its survival, while other mining towns were left behind to become memories of the gold years.

Worthy of attention is the architectural expediency of the structures and the 'fair'-like atmosphere created by the temporary quality of the buildings with their large advertising boards which almost encompassed the buildings themselves.

Braidwood

New South Wales

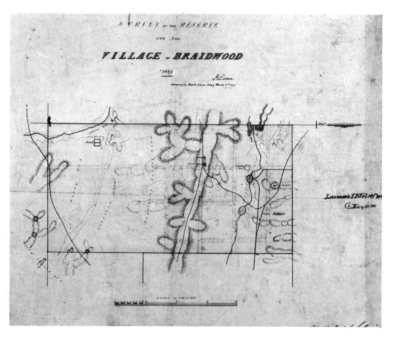

Survey of the Reserve for the Village of Braidwood 1839, T. Larmer. The early huts are shown, and superimposed on the map, with little regard to the topography, are the proposed streets.

Right
The approach to Braidwood is through rugged countryside. Small houses nestle within the broad landscape and form the nucleus of the town.

Explorer Dr Charles Throsby had heard from natives of the existence of a large lake south-west of Lake Bathurst. He fitted out an expedition party and, together with Mr Josh Wild, set out towards the south. On 19 August 1820 Lake George and the district on which the present Federal Capital is now built were discovered.

In October of the same year Governor Macquarie set out in his carriage, from Parramatta, on a tour of the newly discovered lands and nine days of rigorous travel. On reaching plains near a fresh water creek, Macquarie's journal of 28 October reads:
We sat down to dinner today at half past five and after dinner drank a bumper toast to the future settlers of the shores of Lake George, which name I have given to this grand and magnificent sheet of water, in honour of His present Majesty.

Both Throsby and the more noted explorer Hamilton Hume persisted in their endeavours to link Sydney with Jervis Bay by an inland road. After an expedition in 1821 Hume reported that a road could be cut to Batemans Bay further down the coast from Jervis Bay. Such a road, he indicated, would pass through extremely rich lands, which could be opened for settlement and justify the building of the road.

In 1821 Surveyor Harper made sketches of the area and, under the instructions from Surveyor Oxley and Sir Thomas Mitchell, the district was opened up for survey. In 1828 Surveyor Robert Hoddle surveyed the land around the present township of Braidwood.

The first land grant in the Braidwood district was 42,467 acres to the Trustees of the Clergy and School Estate. Other grants followed in 1833. Dr Thomas Braidwood Wilson was granted 2,500 acres on the eastern boundary of the town which he named 'Braidwood Farm'. The Braidwood estate eventually totalled 12,305 acres.

The design and survey of the town was carried out by Surveyor J. Larmer in 1839. The original design was amended, on representations from Dr Wilson, to include a recreation reserve opposite the Court House. The Deputy Surveyor-General wrote:
. . . considerable expense had been incurred by Dr. Wilson in the erection of a handsome building for a Court House, the appearance of the town would be much improved if an area were left about the building that would serve as a place of recreation for the inhabitants.

The amended plans were approved on 4 October 1839 and the first sale of allotments was held on 9 July 1840. Most of the lots were sold.

The town was laid out in a gridiron pattern with the principal streets running north and

Braidwood Court House is neo-Classical in design with Art Nouveau wings—the semi-circular openings are typical of the work of Government Architect Vernon. The Court House stands proudly within its landscaped setting.

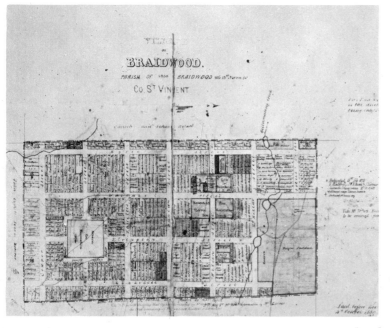

Map of the Village of Braidwood, Parish of Braidwood 1839. The gridiron pattern is softened by reservations for important buildings and parks.

Right
The town of Braidwood slopes gently down the hill, each house and commercial premise bearing a different mass relationship to the next and all contributing to an exciting townscape.

south and the secondary streets east and west. It was a typical surveyor's interpretation of what a town should be and certainly there was an element of civic display with two reserves for recreation, the most important one being the forecourt to the Court House.

The principal streets were Wallace Street, which runs past the Court House and named after the Honourable Mr Hugh Wallace, M.L.C.; Ryrie Street after James Ryrie of 'Arnprior' and this street was the main thoroughfare in the early days. Coghill Street was named after Captain Coghill of 'Bedervale' and Lascelles Street after Dr Francis Lascelles.

The only means of communication from Braidwood in the early days was via Marulan to Sydney and the trip on a bullock dray usually lasted six weeks. To gain a shorter and quicker route, a road to Jervis Bay was again investigated and Dr Wilson, in 1840, induced the Government to construct a new road to the coast. This road became the principal one and was used until gold rush days. A shorter route was then made from Nelligen over the Clyde Mountain from the coast to Braidwood.

Braidwood prospered and grew. The townscape today gives evidence of the Georgian simplicity of the town. A post office was established in 1837 in the small cottage opposite the old mill and mails were carried from Marulan and Jervis Bay, and afterwards from Goulburn, when the stage coach came into use. Most of the buildings were constructed in solid materials, either stone, brick or rubble. The buildings generally had shingled roofs with verandahs sheltering the ground floors. By 1851 the population of the town had risen to 217 persons and by 1856 had climbed to 507 with a further 3,045 in the surrounding district.

In 1852 two prospectors found gold in the Araluen valley near Braidwood. The story is well related in *The Golden Era*.

Early in 1852, two men whose names have not been obtained, travelled along the Deva River from the coast looking for gold. They reached Araluen and though they had carefully searched, could find no trace of the precious metal, and decided to break camp and go back. That night one of them had a vivid dream of finding gold near an old stumpy tree beside the camp, and was so impressed that he dug round the tree and found the gold exactly as he had dreamed.

Other discoveries were made by a shepherd and this turned Braidwood into a boom mining town attracting prospectors from all over the country. The busy Georgian town created by Wilson and his colleagues as a centre for their pastoral pursuits was quickly transformed into a roaring gold town which acquired a new Victorian image with the latest

The Old Mill at Braidwood.

fashionable architectural trappings being secured to the most modest Georgian façades.

The Braidwood fields—Araluen, Bell's Creek, Major's Creek, Jembaicumbene, Mongarlowe, Bombay and many others—proved to be rich. Prospectors in their thousands arrived, especially the Chinese, who numbered about 8,000 at the height of the rush.

Two banks were established at Braidwood: the Australian Joint Stock Bank and the Oriental. Pubs, hotels and hostelries were constructed to cope with the influx with romantic names such as 'The Cottage of Content', 'The Pig and Whistle' and 'The Dog and Stile'.

The surface gold which gave impetus to the town soon petered out, although gold mining continued in the Araluen Valley for many years. River dredging took place with large structures extracting the ore from gravel.

As in all frontier towns, church services were first held in the Court House until permanent churches were built. The Church of England built St Andrew's in 1854 on a site now only marked by elm trees. The present church was built in 1881 and designed by Cyril Blacket.

The Roman Catholic Church was erected in 1856 in the Gothic manner, nobly sited and with a broad flight of steps. The Presbyterians built a simple church with Gothic-pointed windows in 1862, and the Methodist Church was erected in 1856.

The life blood of a Victorian community was its solid determination to have the correct civic institution and no town of respectability could be complete without its churches, schools and gaols, and School of Arts. The School House of granite blocks, consisting of two rooms with a roof of shingle and rooms for housing the headmaster was erected in 1850. It represents the village community at its strongest and typifies so many country towns in Australia.

The Gaol was erected in 1868, a fine stone edifice with symmetrical façade. The Infirmary, a brick, two-storeyed building, was erected in 1860.

The evidence of the booming past is still seen in Braidwood, but now the town has reverted to cater for the needs of a pastoral community. The townscape is controlled by the heavy gridiron pattern of its streets; however, this is relieved to a certain extent by the slight hill upon which the town is sited. The coming in and the going out of Braidwood is always good, a generous feeling of scale is emphasised by the small cottages with shaded verandahs and picket fences which represent the pride of a former era.

Wilcannia

New South Wales

The River Darling is the mainstay of life in the outback of New South Wales. This river was the reason for the town's foundation. Along this muddy stream the river boats hauled bales of wool to Wentworth or to Goolwa in South Australia for shipping overseas. Here ancient gums still stand sentinel. In the background are the remains of the old wharf.

Right
The true beauty and isolation of Wilcannia can be appreciated in this aerial view of the town, the serpentine shape of the river, the sparse vegetation of the surrounding country and the town set out on a gridiron pattern with tree-lined streets.

Imagine a large, muddy gutter running straight for two miles, a few old red gums contorted by the ages standing sentinel to the river and you have the River Darling at Wilcannia.

A drought was largely responsible for the expedition that found a way over the Blue Mountains in New South Wales, and a drought led to the dispatch of a party which discovered the Darling. The river was named in honour of Governor Darling who was most fortunate in his selection of the leader, Captain Charles Sturt of the 39th Regiment. The Captain had with him Mr Hamilton Hume, already distinguished in exploration, Staff-Surgeon McLeod, two soldiers and eight convicts. Following the course of the Macquarie River they discovered, on 4 February 1829, the Darling but unfortunately the water was unfit to drink. Sturt in his journal states:

I shall never forget the cry of amazement or the look of terror with which they cried out to inform me that the river was so salty it was unfit to drink.

They concluded that this saline quality must be derived from near contact with the sea, and anxiously watched for tidal indications. Later the cause was found to be springs in the river's banks.

This muddy gutter, from the 1880s to the turn of the century, was one of the busiest waterways in Australia. M. Cameron, visiting Wilcannia in 1890, described the river scene. *There are several wharves (so-called) which were merely graduated slopes cut out of the river bank, and in the wool season the river, in their vicinity, is thronged with steamers and barges, waiting for or unloading the season's clip, for the bulk of it goes away by water either to Bourke, for Sydney, or to Wentworth, or Goolwa.*

A barge, laden with from 1,200 to 2,000 bales of wool is a pretty sight; and a still more interesting spectacle is a string of 30 or 40 camels, each carrying two bales, proceeding into the town from some far back station.

Wilcannia was founded as a town in 1864. The original intention was to build the town at Moorabin some distance away. The present site was selected by J. Woore who took charge of the district (the Albert) as Commissioner of Crown Lands in 1863.

The first land sales were held in October 1865 when little heed was paid to the surveyors' boundaries. A shanty town seemed to ensue, with the first recorded store constructed from calico on a timber frame.

Gradually buildings of a more permanent nature were built as the town grew.

Nearly every town of some importance had a court house and a gaol. The gaol at Wilcannia was designed in the Classical manner with a central administrative block complete with cells surrounded by high walls with sentry boxes. It was Wilcannia's hope that one day the town would have sufficient population to be called the 'capital of the west'.

Right
There is a quiet brooding, a restfulness, created by the large broadwalks which are stone paved. The recesses of doorways and openings are useful retreats for shade from the afternoon sun.

The *Weekly Advocate* of 22 October 1887 describes the town:
On the evening of the second day, Wilcannia came in sight, over on the western side of the River Darling. The coach crossed on the punt. Barges and steamers were lying along the bank discharging cargo. In one case a pulley was made fast to the branch of a tree, and the shaft of the paddle wheels served as a windlass . . .

We expected to find a place, so far away towards the centre of Australia, in a forlorn and neglected state, but this is not so; instead of scattered galvanised iron shanties we found a concentrated well-built town. The Post Office, Athenaeum, hospital, Court House, Gaol, some of the banks, a few of the hotels, one or two stores, the Public School, the Roman Catholic and the Church of England Churches, are all built of sandstone. The footpaths are kerbed and planted with trees, water is laid on to the town, a boat club is in existence, which has a boat shed in which there are outriggers, eight-oared racing gigs, and other pleasure boats, as those seen on Sydney Harbour.

The town today has not that appearance. The approach to Wilcannia from Sydney is over the bridge, an iron structure with lattice, capable of raising the road level for the river traffic. It is an interesting structure and, like many on the various river systems of New South Wales, it contains wheels and cogs and a whole heap of apparatus for manoeuvring the roadway sections. In the summer the road to this town is over red dusty semi-desert country which borders the open savannah. To see the river, that muddy stream, is a relief, for even that small strip of water offers some comfort. Wilcannia is substantial and, unlike many western towns which are built from timber frames with a variety of material cladding, it was built for permanence with stone and brick. Most of the roofs have iron sheeting and this gives a consistency and tends to unify the architecture of the town.

The major buildings are the pubs and the public administration headquarters, gaol, churches and schools.

The pubs are built solidly out of stone with iron lace verandahs surrounding them. Gum trees have been planted around to afford additional shade from the fierce heat of summer.

Buildings of quite good proportion and civic presence are the Post Office, an edifice of three arches forming an arcade, with the central arcade raised to form a pediment. Next to this building, by contrast, is a late-Victorian building with an iron lace verandah which gives strength to the former, giving the base building solidity. The Council Office is a simple yet dignified building. Although modest in its proportions, it fits well into the streetscape.

102

The bridge at Wilcannia is one of many drawbridges over the River Darling. In former days the raising of the bridge was necessitated by the wool barges, often laden to great heights, which had to gain clearance.

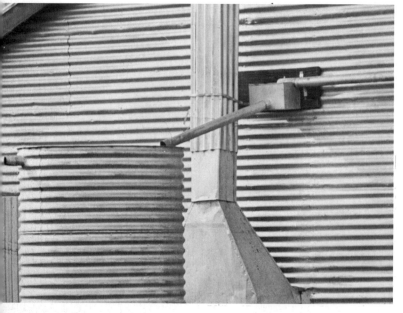

Masonry is not needed to create good architecture. Here the consistent use of galvanised iron makes an interesting composition of flat wall surfaces contrasting with cylinders and triangular forms. It is almost Cubist in its content.

Right
Main street in Wilcannia.

At one stage Wilcannia was an important town and administrative centre, and, in accordance with its position, was given a gaol and a court house. The combined Court House and Police Station is a reasonably proportioned building with central pavilion with flanking side pavilions of a single-storey scale.

The central pavilion is surmounted by a triangular pediment, in fact a gable, in which bulls-eye ventilators and the windows have been symmetrically placed. A verandah runs around the skirt of the building. It is not the architecture which is surprising in this far-western town, but the permanence of the structure and the masonry, which is accurately joined and carefully put together. It is unlike anything that one would expect for such a remote town.

The Gaol, which is adjacent, bears the formidable expression typical of such an establishment. Built from ashlar walls that surround the compound, it is punctuated only by block houses with hip roofs. There is an equally forbidding central block. The only relief in the architecture is some decorative ventilators and gable ends.

In the suburbs the houses vary from shanties to former mansions, but in all cases the architecture has the flavour of the climate. The basic house unit is a square box encircled by verandahs filled in with fly gauze. The covering-in by gauze results in less of a three-dimensional quality to these houses and diminishes the architectural quality of many. However, when the mullions are painted white, a gentle rhythm is created between void and solid. In the main street of Wilcannia there are two anachronisms. These are the Plaza theatre and the general store beside the theatre. Constructed as if they were intended for a Bauhaus exercise, they appear as cardboard versions of the latest Art Deco architecture of the capital cities. And yet they have vitality, a 'tongue-in-cheek' attitude towards the fashions in architecture which may have eluded them in philosophical terms.

From Wilcannia the road goes on and on into the flatness of the horizon. There is no change to the scenery until the small red hills of Broken Hill break the monotony.

There are 'high style' architectural contributions in Wilcannia which are mainly variations upon the Victorian theme. This portico expressed in masonry has a dignified expression and is an extension of the verandah theme whilst the building next to it revives the modulation of the verandah column.

Right
A great majority of the buildings in Wilcannia were built in stone. This building now deserted, has a formal composition of circular-headed windows contrasting with completely square proportioned shop fronts. The massive proportions of this shop contrasts with the single-storied terrace housing beside.

Silverton

New South Wales

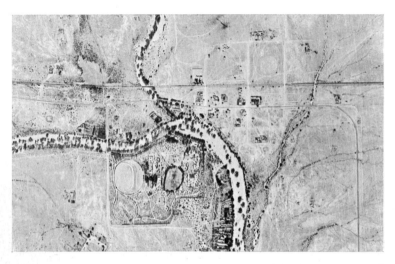

Aerial photograph. Only a few
remains of Silverton exist. The marks
of man, the natural drainage systems,
can be detected as well as the evidence of
the pride which was once Silverton.

Right
Most of the imagery in Silverton is
poetry activated by desolation and
isolation. Although the ruins of this
church have no architectural importance,
the proportions are exaggerated in this
desert atmosphere especially where
verticals contrast sharply against the
never ending horizon.

Over
The town is almost completely
destroyed and yet there is a wonderful
feeling of space created by the
juxtaposition of these buildings. The little
church, simplistic in its neo-Gothic
expression, pays lip service to civilisation,
especially in the carved valence boards.
The church almost echoes its architecture
in the distance like a shattering reverberation.

It isn't really a town at all now, but it was and it still retains a ghostly quality. The town has an air of extreme melancholia as though suffering the result of a holocaust, or the ravages of war.

Silverton, originally called Umberumberka, did have better days, and at one stage it was a bustling, vital town. The area was discovered by the explorer Charles Sturt in 1844 but it was not until 1876, when silver-lead ore was discovered at Thackaringa by Paddy Green, that any authentic information was collected. As a result prospectors came from all parts of Australia to share the riches from this inhospitable area of dust and dune.

The country around the Barrier Ranges and Silverton is extremely flat desert with only small undulations. Stunted trees on the landscape, and the general aridity, lead to despair. The country changes in colour from soft greys and greens of the fertile fringes to burnt oranges and reds of the desert. There is a gentleness in the desert colours which take dramatic effects in the evening light. There is little water here, even in a good season. Essentially it is hostile to man but in this scorched land miners trudged to try their luck.

No serious claims seem to have been made until 1880 when gold-bearing lodes were discovered near Thackaringa which increased the population of the town to 200 persons almost overnight.

A year later Silverton was surveyed and another rush began. Silverton was recognised as a town on 17 September 1880. Richard O'Connell was sent in charge of the police. Amongst his many duties was Acting Clerk of Petty Sessions, Mining Registrar, and Wardens Clerk. The first influx of people took place in 1883 and in September of that year the population had risen to 250. By 1884 the silver fervour had gripped the town and the census recorded the population at 1,745. Stories of incredible rich lodes spread and when it became known that discoveries were continuing to be made the population swelled to 3,000. This was the zenith of Silverton. It was a busy, bustling mining town, filled with miners and companies with 'wildcat' schemes who had obtained their information from 'experts'.

All had the same ambition—to make money. Silverton had hardly been prepared for the influx. There were a few hotels and a store, but the increase of population was far ahead of any provisions for its reception. Essentially it was a tent city mixed up with mining shafts and semi-permanent buildings. Those who possessed tents were envied by many who lacked even this provision. For many, to spend the night on the billiard table of a hotel was a luxury. In

The Municipal Chambers were
constructed in 1889, the foundation
stone being laid by H. Brown, Mayor.
It was unfortunate that this was the year
the mines closed and with them,
Silverton.

Over
A twentieth century landscape
—what a fitting reminder!

The History of Broken Hill it stated: 'Many is the man of affluence today who was only too glad to dump on the floor with a "bluey" or camp alongside the creek with the great unknown.'

Food and every commodity advanced in price. Bread was 2s. per 4 lb loaf, meat 7d a lb and vegetables could not be had at any price. Water cost 6d per bucket and better-quality water brought forty-five miles from Mingary in South Australia was 1s. per bucket. All stores had to be supplied from Adelaide, via Terowie. The journey lasted twenty-one days and freight charges were £7 a ton.

Sydney people travelling to Silverton caught the train to Hay and then endured three days on a Cobb & Co. coach over the black soil plains. Those making the journey from Adelaide left the train at Terowie and then journeyed by coach.

In the heyday of Silverton there were uninterrupted lines of shops, mostly weatherboard with stone chimneys, with verandahs sheltering the façades. There were the more opulent buildings such as the Bank of Australia built from bluestone, which opened in December 1885 and cost £1500. After the boom it was sold for £50. There were butchers' shops, saddleries, hotels, greengrocers, mining agents—all housed comfortably in what may appear, if it remained today, a movie set for a wild western film. The civic pride of Silverton was expressed in the Municipal Chambers, deserted on the year of its completion. The foundation stone records '1889, H. Brown, Mayor' and in that year the mine closed down and with it Silverton.

The mines which were the life-blood of Silverton were numerous. There was the Umberumberka Mine, about two miles from Silverton, opened in 1882, and from which 500 tons of ore were extracted. The Day Dream Mine, about fourteen miles from Broken Hill, raised 96,000 tons of ore. The mine was continued until 1888 and then the machinery was dismantled and the coke sold to the Proprietary Company at Broken Hill. Purnamoota, the Pinnacles and Pilgrim Mine were all successful operations which used Silverton as a housing and commercial centre.

Towards the end of September 1883 a boundary rider, Charles Rasp, was struck by the mineral appearance of Broken Hill within the Mt Gipps Station. In conjunction with Messrs Poole and James, contractors on the station, Rasp pegged off and applied for mineral leases on Broken Hill. Rasp mentioned this to his manager, Mr George McCulloch, who was part-owner of the property. Both men believed that the bluff end was tin, and accordingly pegged off blocks which took in the entire hill. These blocks were applied for in the names of Geo. McCulloch, George Urquhart and G. A. M. Lind, the latter two being overseer and storekeeper of the Mt Gipps run. Two more blocks were applied for and the total of seven blocks secured the two miles of known reef which was then amalgamated into one private company under the name of 'The Broken Hill Mining Company' the members of which were: George McCulloch; Charles Rasp; Philip Charley; David James; James Poole; George Urquhart and G. A. M. Lind.

Each of the above seven contributed £70. After further surface prospecting, exposing larger bodies of comparatively lower-grade carbonate of lead ore, Lind retired from the Company. Rasp and McCulloch took up his interest in equal proportions. After eight months Urquhart also sold his interest to the Company. It was then necessary to reform the Company consisting of fourteen shares.

Things went very slowly at Broken Hill at the start but, as the history of Broken Hill goes, the mine was enormously successful and won riches beyond all dreams.

With the rise of Broken Hill, Silverton fell into ruin and disrepair and finally became a ghost town. There is only one store in the town today. On the far side of the railway track there are four buildings in various stages of ruin. One of these is the school house, on the rise beyond is the Methodist Church, and two other buildings are houses girded by salt bush.

Bendigo

Victoria

The Bendigo Goverment Camp in 1853. Reproduced from sketch of J. A. Paton, Resident Commissioner.

Pall Mall in 1855. The roads are still mud and there are many temporary looking buildings; however, the 'Victoria Hotel' and S. Jones stores appear more permanent structures.

Right
Pall Mall in 1905. The magnificent fountain in the centre of the street is surrounded by nymphs and to the right foreground a gold mine is still operating in the centre of town. The Town Hall can be seen centre of the picture with the Law Courts to the right.

Of all towns in Australia Bendigo is the most outstanding example of the 'boom town'. The word 'boom' has been coined by architects and historians to classify the period between 1870 and 1890 when the Victorian architectural style was at its most flamboyant, and civic pride expressed itself in statues, fountains, bandstands and grand town halls.

It was a period of prosperity which coincided with architectural eclecticism and intellectual escapes such as 'the Battle of the Styles', the complete floundering in an attempt to decide which style, either Gothic or Renaissance, was to win the Victorian taste and mind.

And yet, in retrospect, the creation of a unique style was achieved perhaps unknowingly. The Victorian who perceived his buildings in either a Gothic manner or a Renaissance or rural Italianate way, and who strove with complete honesty and sincerity to copy and to initiate buildings of the past—adapting only where necessary to suit new planning requirements—found that he had in fact created something unique.

Such was the position with planning towns in the Victorian age; the gridiron pattern was well established, it represented ease of construction, subdivision, access and servicing. It gave the possibilities of incorporating vistas and parks easily and monotony could be broken in a variety of ways.

Professor R. B. Mowat in *The Victorian Age* summarised the Victorian attitude of life which influenced the towns and cities they built and the houses and buildings they used.

It was their belief in progress which chiefly distinguished Victorians from those of other ages. They did not hold (as many people in the eighteenth century believed themselves) that they were at the apex of civilization. They were pleased with their scientific discoveries and inventions, their missionary and philanthropic efforts, but they also thought they could do better and that subsequent generations would do better still. They took it for granted that there would be progress not just in this and that direction, but generally throughout society. "Progress" was not a concept of particular improvements though they were worked for and welcomed, but of an even further advance towards the divine perfection.

There is a fair degree of gigantism associated with the Victorian age—which expresses itself so adequately in towns and buildings. The people who shed some light on this lustrous period are people like Acton, Arnold, Browning, Carlyle, Darwin, Dickens, Disraeli, Eliot, Faraday, Hardy, Huxley, Macaulay, Newman, Florence Nightingale, Rodin, Tennyson and Trollope. They give persistent fascination to the time. Coupled with these, the Australian image was

This view can be identified with the previous photograph by the location of the fountain. The consistency of the street architecture of Bendigo remaining from the nineteenth century can be appreciated.

Right
Decadent, architecturally insane and opulent buildings build up rich architectural street patterns in Bendigo. The Bendigo Arcade on the left has its entrance emphasised by an Indian Stupa form whilst the National Bank façade has the first floor well out of scale with the ground floor and, if that was not sufficient, the architect decided that the whole would be more appropriate as a triumphal arch. The M.L.C. building adjacent appears more sober by comparison.

being fashioned out of the remnants of a discordant society by people like Lawson, Paterson, Roberts, Streeton, Conder, Clarke and others. It was a period giving impetus to the economy, and when indulgences in any extravagance were permitted. It truly was a golden age.

The name of Bendigo was synonymous with gold. The discovery of gold there in November 1851 immediately gave birth to the town. The lands around Bendigo were part of the Ravenswood run owned by Messrs Gibson and Fenton. These gentlemen had ridden out to the Bendigo Creek to inspect their flocks and on their return stopped to spell their horses at the junction of Golden Valley with the main stream. While they were sitting they noticed something gleaming in a tussock of grass amongst the roots of a tree which flood waters had laid bare. It was gold. By the next day the story had leaked out and thus began the rush to Bendigo.

As a result of the discovery of gold, Melbourne and Geelong were almost deserted. The yield from the Bendigo field in 1851 was officially stated to be 200,000 oz, and in 1852, 475,857 oz.

Vast areas of ground were turned over to bed rock, whole forests of great ironbark trees with dense underwood disappeared. The range of hills dividing the city proper from Ironbark was so densely timbered that no view could be obtained of the Bendigo Valley, and this proved a useful place to rob unsuspecting prospectors. The town of Bendigo began to grow amidst the bustle of people anxious to claim their rewards, with the streets being dusty affairs, and the buildings temporary.

Public buildings and buildings of permanence started to evolve. The first chapel, originally a tent, was built in 1852. The foundation stone of the Masonic Hall was laid in 1856. In the same year the Roman Catholic Church was started. At the beginning of 1856 preparations were being made to open a theatre known as Coleman's Criterion. It was 100 feet long by twenty-five feet, widening to forty feet, and consisted of pits and stalls with a huge chandelier hanging from the ceiling.

Many of the important buildings of Bendigo were designed by William Charles Vahland, a German architect, who had been attracted to the gold fields in 1854. Together with three companions he came to Bendigo to try his luck but had no success. Instead he obtained work as a carpenter and later opened up shop in Bridge Street. In 1857 he established an architectural practice which eventually secured the most important buildings, except those

118

The Town Hall was designed by
W. C. Vahland in 1872. The strange
proportions of the building were no
doubt due to the incorporation of the
former town hall into the new design.
The architecture is in Italian Renaissance
vocabulary. The design is vigorous and an
excellent example of Vahland's work.
Among his other work in Bendigo is the
Hospital 1858–59, the Benevolent
Asylum and the Mechanics' Institute.

Right
Detail of the ground floor of
Vahland's Town Hall. The streets
around the central point in Bendigo are
tree-lined and extremely urban, more
cityscape in appearance than any other
country town in Australia.

carried out by the Public Works Department. His work included the Benevolent Asylum and
Hospital; School of Mines; Mechanics' Institute; Town Hall; Masonic Hall; Princess Theatre;
Synagogue; the Australasian, Commercial, Colonial and National Banks; the Alexandra
Foundation at Charing Cross, and a number of private houses.

His most affluent work must be the Town Hall. Vahland had stood for Council and held
office between 1869 and 1872. During this time it became evident that a new town hall had
to be built. In accordance with his ethics, Vahland resigned but it was not until ten years later
in 1883 that sufficient funds were found.

Plans were drawn up for a magnificent edifice, which incorporated the existing town hall,
for the cost of £30,000. The building was a florid example of the Italianate-cum-French and
formed an asymmetrical composition with the clock tower. The tower is expressed in a
truncated pyramid capped with a delicate lace parapet not unlike the grand details of ironwork
used in the Sydney Town Hall. The roof line of the main hall was similarly treated with iron
finials so that it would merge with the sky. The interiors are good and varied and the
succession of spaces indicates a complete control of the plasticity of architecture. Particularly
interesting is the plaster work in the town hall proper which included palmette motifs in the
ceiling panels. Painted panels were incorporated in the plaster niches in the walls expressing
music and poetry and other muses. Unfortunately some of these have been destroyed in
redecorating.

Rivalling the Town Hall were the Public Offices, 1883–87, and the Law Courts, 1892–96,
both designed by W. G. Watson of the Public Works Department. The Public Offices are
more restrained than Vahland's work, and perhaps better architecture. There is less striving and
less conflict, less ambiguity of structure, less tricks for an architectural effect. Like the Town
Hall, the Post Office is also asymmetrical in its composition, with the clock tower on one
corner counterpoised by a small pavilion at the other end. The centre of the composition is
articulated by a small projection of the elevation with curved mansard roof. The rhythm of
the fenestration is even, consistent and well proportioned, and each floor is separated by a
continuous balcony course interspersed with Palladian Balustrades. The ironwork is more
restrained than that of the Town Hall. However, in the final analysis, it may be decided that
an expression of virility, capturing the virility of the Victorian period, is better than more
subtle pieces of scholarly interpretation of Renaissance architecture.

Above
The upper landing acts as a vestibule to the Supreme Court and is handsomely detailed. The floor has mosaic tiling of strong colour whilst the plasterwork is softly coloured. The doors to the courtroom are constructed from cedar and to achieve a symmetry of composition, a false door balances the door to the Court on the right hand side.

The Supreme Court is lit by gas chandeliers. Among the etched ornament of the main windows appear names of famous British judges and on the upper panels appear the equivalent Victorian personalities. The interior of the chamber is carefully modelled with fine plasterwork. The woodwork throughout is cedar except for the judges' bench which is walnut.

Right
Exterior of Courts.

Over left
One of the most magnificent Victorian hotels in Australia is the 'Shamrock Hotel.' It is more London than Bendigo in its superstructure; however the verandah appears almost as a skirt which makes the remaining structure float above it.

Over right
The street façades of a great deal of Bendigo consist of restrained Victorian buildings, not unlike some parts of London. Not all of Bendigo has the same flamboyance as Pall Mall.

View of Bendigo from the Tower. Below can be seen the public buildings, previously described, set in the tree-lined streets which give almost a park-like setting.

The Law Courts are the last of the Grand Victorian Buildings, and most probably the best. The building is French Renaissance in style and is symmetrically designed. It is almost square in plan and each corner is emphasised by a truncated mansard roof capped in a delicate manner and finished with a cast iron finial. The roof line is extraordinarily good with a multiplicity of shapes: curved and straight roofs, chimneys and finials, and the whole being capped off with delicate iron lace.

The splendour of the courts is within and expresses a mastery of space. The upper landing acts as a vestibule to the Supreme Court and is delicately detailed with applied arcading and engaged columns. The order chosen for the courts was Corinthian with a free interpretation of column bases which tend to be more florid and distinctly Victorian. The interior nevertheless has a restraint which is sometimes uncommon for this period. The Court room itself is well proportioned and it glows with polished timber and brass. Most of the timber is cedar except for some panels of walnut from which the bench is constructed.

Bendigo is hardly a town, it is an important Victorian city, and perhaps can be seen as the final accomplishment and desire and aspiration of every country town. It has the elements of a small town, but the architectural works are executed in much splendour, and it is not difficult to feel that you are in a city of importance with the atmosphere and vigour of the gold rush.

Maldon

Victoria

The general appearance of Maldon is one of trees and the impression which it leaves is the integration between urbanscape and landscape. The main street bends and twists, not at all typical of the majority of country towns in Australia which are laid out on a gridiron pattern prescribed by Sir Thomas Mitchell, Surveyor-General of New South Wales.

Right
From the main street, the country is always visibly present and yet there is a distinct visual separation between country and town. The surrounding hills visually form a background to the street. The rhythm of trees, either in the landscape or the street, are picked up in staccato fashion by the slender verandah posts. Maldon is entirely a verandahed town and this is a rare sight in Australia today.

Maldon originally was a gold mining township situated some ninety miles south-west of Melbourne at the foot of Mt Tarrangower in central Victoria. The history of the Maldon district before the discovery of gold in 1853 is obscure. It is known that Major Mitchell's exploration party across northern and western Victoria in 1836 went within the area of Mt Tarrangower. The squatters followed and established themselves along the Loddon River Flats. There were two principal runs—Cairn Curran and Tarrangower, the licences of these runs expiring in the late seventies.

In 1853 a certain Captain John G. Mechosk found gold on the Tarrangower run and so the rush started.

Mr William Howitt, an English traveller and writer, describes the story of the big rush in an article called 'Land, Labour and Gold', published in 1855.

There is a new rush, and a violent one, thousands and thousands of the people who have come up here from the Ovens are now off again, helter skelter, down to a place called the Porcupine, from the Porcupine Inn, beyond Bendigo. These crowds will in less than a fortnight have travelled upwards of three hundred miles after new rushes. By all accounts the diggings of the Porcupine, or Bryant's Ranges, are totally destitute of water; a hot, burnt up place, and however rich it may be, will be torn up long before these people, about 5,000 in number, can get there. It lies between Bendigo and Forest Creek, and not more than 60 miles from Ballarat, so that if it proved good, 80,000 could be upon it in less than a fortnight.

As an alluvial field, Maldon was only of secondary importance, but comes a close second in rivalling Bendigo as the richest quartz mine in Victoria. After the original find of gold by Captain Mechosk, the next most significant find was by McNulty and Hurly who chanced upon an outcrop hidden in a clump of timber. Other sensational discoveries followed: Eagle Hawk, Bell's Reef and the Beehive in 1854; German, Nuggetty, Victoria, and Lisle's Reefs in 1855; Linscott's and Parkin's Reefs in 1856.

As soon as the Government realised that the Tarrangower gold diggings showed signs of permanency, Surveyor John Templeton was instructed to select a site for a town and this was completed in 1854. More detailed surveys were carried out by Adair in 1856. The town plan is quite irregular and not like the more orderly subdivisions which relied on a gridiron pattern. The reason for the irregularity is not known. George McArthur, local historian, recorded:

A detail of a carriage entrance through one of the shops. The stables were very much a part of life in country towns and access was generally gained through rear lanes.

Right

Civic pride is expressed in Maldon's paved streets and wide overhanging verandahs. All these contribute to make Maldon one of Australia's best-preserved towns of the late nineteenth century.

Over left

The curving main street at Maldon is full of subtleties. Especially worth noting is the 'good manners' in the architectural detailing of parapet walls which are kept at a constant height.

The township's unshapeliness in the form of acute and obtuse angles has given endless trouble and perplexity to all architects and builders from the first to the last. I have not seen anywhere a town so irregularly formed.

Adair is credited with giving the township the name of Maldon after a town in Essex, England. The first Government land sale was held on 16 November 1856.

During its early days, Maldon was controlled by a Resident Gold Commissioner with a small supporting police force of six members who maintained law and order on the gold fields. In 1858 this form of government was superseded by the proclamation of Maldon as a municipality, and the government of the town was handed over to an elected body of councillors.

By 1859 the population was growing at a rapid rate and during the succeeding years the main town buildings were erected. These included the market place, erected in 1859 from bluestone, quite an unusual and sophisticated building for its time. The building of the market place no doubt resulted from the decision of the councillors of the rival city of Castlemaine to build a market. It was erected for the cost of £1,250 and was today's version of the supermarket. It had booths set up inside for various retailers who sold on a cooperative shopping basis. Fruits and vegetables, and goods from cotton reels to turkeys could be bought amid the bustle of eager shoppers and the colourful people of the mining era. The bluestone market building had circular-headed windows and openings. The entrance was surmounted by a pedimented shaft which may have been intended for a future clock. This building survived as a market until 1866 when, by decision of council, it was converted into shire offices with provisions for a concert hall at the rear.

A hospital was also founded at about the same time as the market, the money being raised by public subscription. Two long brick wards were constructed to separately house male and female patients and the whole was completed by a formal composition of a two-storey ward between the two previous pavilions.

The Court House was erected in 1861 and a Post and Telegraph Office in 1870 after many years of temporary premises. All these were built with Victorian pride and were necessary features of the prospering Victorian town.

After the gold rush the town had to face many problems concerned with essential services such as forming roads and footways, erecting bridges, constructing water channels and providing

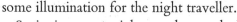

Maldon's suburbs are restrained and unified by picket fences which tie together diverse architectural themes.

The Maldon Hospital is a grand edifice designed in Palladian composition.

Right
The virility of the gold rush is seen in hotels such as the 'Maldon Hotel' consisting of a street façade composed of semicircular and segmental arches in gentle balance and the whole tied together by a strong colour. 'Shakespeare House' picks up the same mood as the hotel and develops the general theme further along the street.

some illumination for the night traveller.

Sanitation was a nightmare but gradually a system of collection and removal, or the use of deep pit latrines, was instituted and the problem overcome.

The councillors in 1862 thought up the idea of increasing revenue for road expenditure by placing toll gates across the main road at Muckleford. But public outcry killed this scheme completely. Slate paving stones were laid in 1866 along the High Street footpath between Spring and Fountain Streets, and much of this pavement is still in good condition.

It is amazing to find the strength and expression of Victorian confidence in the country towns at this period. Many of the features of the towns which we enjoy today were carried out as an expression of civic pride. Tasmanian gums were planted to shade the streets in 1867 and bridges erected to cope with the increasing traffic.

The Civic Centre or Gardens was the place of rest, a place for the promenading of the town's ladies in their cotton frocks and new bonnets on a Sunday after church, or resting after the heat of the day. On occasions, such as the marriage of Edward, Prince of Wales, to Princess Alexandra, a huge crowd collected. Addresses were printed on silk fabric and two oak seedlings from Windsor Park, England, were planted to commemorate the occasion. In 1902 the Civic Centre resounded with the excitement and the cheering of the Coronation of King Edward VII and a pageant was held to celebrate the occasion. On Saturday nights there was shopping and this was the occasion for getting out and enjoying oneself. Brass bands played in the park and there was a feeling of gaiety and social oneness.

Maldon is one of the most picturesque of the gold rush towns today. The irregular allotments and street pattern—the curse of the surveyors and builders—give a romantic charm to the town. There is an elegance about the streets created by the slender cast iron columns which support the wide, overhanging verandahs. The scale of the streets is predominantly one-storey and the parapets of the shops are raised in order to conceal any roof structure. It is essentially a 'frontier' town in this respect, with usually an appearance of the temporary but reinforced with the most permanent looking hotels of robust proportions and vigorous ornamentation. Such a building is the 'Maldon Hotel', which is crowned by a semi-circular pediment and flanked by two miniature obelisks, with the circular theme repeated in the archways to the yards. Superimposed on this façade is a cast iron verandah of extreme delicacy concealing a multitude of architectural sins and giving the building the necessary

Along the fringes of the town the
evidence of the gold rush can still be
seen in the large mullock heaps and
small miners' cottages standing in ruins on
the surrounding landscape.

Right
There is much to learn in the town
plan of Maldon—the leafy streets, the
lightness and airiness of the verandahs as
well as the irregular street pattern all of
which give diversity to the urban
structure.

lightness which it would otherwise not possess. Much of the Victorian heaviness in architectural treatment can be seen in country towns where the verandahs have been foolishly stripped from the façades and, more often than not, replaced by coarse metal awnings.

Around the outskirts of Maldon are merchants' houses representing the full flood of Victorian eclecticism. They are nevertheless restrained in their mass and form. They are essentially vernacular houses with a central hallway and rooms leading to either side. The roofs are iron and in most cases the houses are sheltered by a front verandah. It was in the verandah detailing that the Victorian cast iron founder and joiner found his most florid expression. These houses, either small or large, are neatly placed in a suburban setting—they are essentially urban in their character, in contrast with the broader vernacular of the country homestead. The outbuildings, sheds and stores which create a strong rural character are replaced here by picket fences, hedges and urban garden trappings.

There was a common treatment throughout the 'new world' during this time and the similarity between American mid-west country towns and the Australian equivalent cannot be ignored. Maldon has the consciousness of being a town steeped in the history of the gold fields. It has the feeling that the townspeople are conscious of their heritage, and the tourist potential which may accrue from its preservation.

Beechworth

Victoria

A contemporary picture showing gold-seekers travelling to a gold field. Chinese miners travelling by foot in a long single file were a common sight in the gold rushes. From Nan Kivell Collection by courtesy National Library, Canberra.

Right
The remains of the Chinese cemetery at Beechworth. The thousands of Chinese formed their own community which was complete with Joss House and shops and, for many years, the Chinese community figured prominently in the town's early history.

The country around Beechworth rolls and tumbles with large outcrops of rock covered with lichen and shaded with stunted trees. Ferns and silver-trunked eucalypt groves soften this landscape. Before gold was discovered in this area the country was frequented by shepherds. James Meldrum, shepherd overseer for David and John Reid whose possessions included Yachandanda No 1, Barnawartha and Woorajay, spent much of his time fossicking and on one of his trips he found traces of gold in the Spring Creek area. Another of the Reid Brothers' shepherds, Howell, found fourteen pounds weight of gold in this area. So the news leaked out and the rush started. Along the roads the miners trudged to the new fields. A newcomer wrote in his journal:

You would be amused to see the almost endless trains of bullock drays and diggers' carts on the roads. The drays are covered with canvas awnings and drawn by eight or ten bullocks each . . . The diggers' carts are piled with all sorts of diggers' apparatus—shovels, sieves, cradles, iron buckets, picks, axes and the like. Behind hang whole heaps of pans, pannikins, kettles, and iron pots, with a sprinkling of frying pans. Upon the rest of the cargo lie beds and bedding and often two or three women and some children.

A calico and canvas settlement was erected with great speed and, as we are told by contemporary observers, this occurred almost overnight with the town straggling the ridges on the present site of Beechworth.

On 1 May 1853, Lieutenant-Governor La Trobe visited the diggings and named them the May Day Hills. He instructed the Government Surveyor, Smythe, to survey allotments and lay out the principal streets of the town. Beechworth was renamed by Smythe after his home town in Leicestershire, England, and was proclaimed a town on 1 July 1853.

Gradually the tent city, with more permanent occupancy of storekeepers and hostelries, turned into a timber one with slab huts and weatherboard cottages; shingle roofs replaced the temporary calico, shops displayed large signs to sell their wares and hotels were shaded with large verandahs which tended to keep the feet dry in winter and the heat off in summer.

The society in the early gold fields left much to be desired. James Bonwich, a school inspector, visited the fields and complained of the rudeness of mere living and the want of civilised appliances, the constant jostling of sexes together in confined spaces and the 'betrayal of scenes more properly requiring retirement'. Drunken exhibitions were constant and gambling, consisting mainly of bagatelle, dominoes, and two-up were common games,

The gaol at Beechworth is like a romantic castle having the appearance of a fortified town such as mediaeval Carcassonne. The building was, however, far from romantic in its use—it once held the famous Ned Kelly and many of his gang. Today it is still used as a corrective institution.

Right
To walk along the main street in Beechworth is a leafy experience. Most of the buildings are constructed in stone or brick and are either single or two storey. Their expression is essentially vernacular excepting the important buildings such as the Gold Office or the Post Office which have pretensions to a 'high' style.

frequented both by Europeans and Chinese. Mrs Charles Clancy visited the diggings and kept a diary of the early scenes:

The stores, which are distinguished by a flag, are numerous and well stocked. A new style of lodging and boarding house is in great vogue. It is a tent filled up with stringy-bark couches, ranged down each side of the tent, leaving a narrow passage in the middle. The lodgers are supplied with mutton, damper and tea, three times a day, for the charge of 5s. a meal and 5s. for the bed; this is by the week—a casual guest may pay double and as 18 inches is an average considered ample width to sleep in, a tent 24 feet long will bring in a good return to the owner.

Adding to the colour and vigour of the tent town were the many thousands of Chinese who swarmed over the gold fields. Beechworth had its permanent Chinese camp, complete with Joss House, shops and cafes, and for many years the Chinese community played a prominent role in the town's early affairs. In Beechworth today there are the remains of many hundreds of graves and the Chinese ceremonial burning towers still to be seen in the cemetery.

1855 was a memorable year in the history of Beechworth. Not only was it the year that Captain O'Hara Bourke arrived as Officer in Charge of Police, but it was also the year in which the first copy of the *Ovens and Murray Advertiser* was printed and the erection of a water-powered flour mill completed.

An interesting glimpse of the town as it appeared at this stage is given in the memoirs of Superintendent Sadlier, a police officer, who was stationed at Beechworth during the fifties. He refers to the town as being in a 'very unfinished state' the shops, all of which stayed open at night, were mostly canvas with wooden frontages. Both banks, the Oriental and the Victorian, did their business in small two-roomed cottages, while the government buildings consisted of a row of slab huts lined with baize.

With the introduction of a town council, public utilities were organised in 1857. A permanent town water supply was instituted, a fire brigade formed and contracts were let for the sub-treasury building (now the police station), police offices (now the forestry office), and the Athenaeum Hall. Of all these projects the Athenaeum Hall was the only one erected within that year. Other work completed during that year was the laying out and building of the Chinese camp on the high ground above Lake Sambell. Here a miniature town was set out, complete with streets thirty feet wide, and included in the development were Chinese

Above & right
The architecture of Beechworth is a contrast between lace verandahs and the solid Victorian façades. Much of the Victorian architecture in Beechworth has been carefully preserved and it possesses a unity and architectural consistency which many other towns in Australia lack. The 'Commercial Hotel' is one of the most opulent in town. 'Cawthray's Empire Hotel' has the same treatment.

theatres, restaurants, boarding houses, shops and a Joss House.

1857 is recorded as a year of almost continual blasting, building and road making, with its citizens, during the winter, in Wellington boots struggling desperately to negotiate the almost impassable roads and footpaths.

In the next six years the old Post Office was replaced by a stone one and in 1859 the present Gaol was commenced, this being completed by the following year at a cost of £1,000. By 1862 there was nightly entertainment, either plays, operas or vaudeville shows of one kind or another. Circuses came and went during most of the year and the English Eleven visited Beechworth, played, and won against a team of twenty-two local cricketers. The Beechworth Progress Association said in 1892 in *An Illustrated Guide to Beechworth and Vicinity* that the temporary buildings resulting from the gold rush had now been replaced, the streets had been 'metalled' and footpaths formed.

Public buildings were constructed. 'Of these' said the Progress Association proudly, 'the most noteworthy, and of which the towns-people are justly proud, are the Hospital, Benevolent Asylum, and Public Library, which were all founded by private enterprise soon after Beechworth was established as a town, while the Post Office, Gaol, Law Courts and Lunatic Asylum, demonstrate the appreciation of Beechworth by the Government, not only as an important district centre, but also as a site unrivalled as a sanatarium.'

The Ovens Benevolent Asylum, now called the Ovens and Murray Home, was opened in 1863 and sited on a hill overlooking the town. It was designed with a russet and white brick façade in a colonial Dutch manner. Unfortunately the effect was destroyed when a new building was built in front.

The Beechworth Mental Hospital, by contrast, is a huge Italianate building, heavy in its proportions and prison-like in its appearance. It represented security to both the townspeople and the inmates, and a secure form of trade for the grocers and shopkeepers.

There were five courts held in Beechworth—the Police, Petty Sessions, Mining Board, County and Supreme Court. In 1863, Beechworth was proclaimed a municipality. It has not changed very much from the late seventies; the streets have most of the buildings intact and today it represents a complete Victorian town. What other town could boast county gaol, post and telegraph offices, savings bank, court house, land office, gold office and treasury, warden's office, police station, railway station, state school, municipal buildings

The Post Office at Beechworth is a handsome building and terminates the street turning well with its robust clock tower. The elegance of the Victorian street architecture can be appreciated, especially in the consistency of scale created by double-storey buildings with verandahs.

Right
The main street of Beechworth. In the centre of the street can be seen the 'Commercial Hotel,' recently restored.

such as a town hall, council chambers, public library (with over 4,753 volumes) and fire brigade station?

The original Beechworth Hospital, whose foundation stone was laid in 1856, now stands in ruins. Its grand façade looks like a gateway to an English park as if it had always been designed as a ruin or some great playful landscape thing. It was designed in the Palladian manner.

The Shire Hall has little architectural merit and is typical of many municipal buildings of the 1880s. By far the most interesting building is the Gaol with its fairy castle-like appearance. Conical towers with octagonal roofs are really the only outward form expressed and these tend to obliterate the real menace behind its walls. The building was constructed from granite blocks which twice held the bushranger Ned Kelly. In 1926 it became a reformatory prison and in 1951 a training prison.

Beechworth ceased to be a boom town in the 1880s as mining declined and with it many of the town's industries. Tourism is one of the important industries in the town today and visitors can tread the interesting streets or descend the valley and inspect the Powder Works which have recently been restored.

Port Fairy

Victoria

Aerial view of Port Fairy

Right
The first sight of Port Fairy when
approached from the western district
is a strip of Norfolk Island Pine trees.
The surrounding countryside, composed of
verdant rolling hills with grazing
cattle, is particularly beautiful.

The little town of Port Fairy, known to the Aborigines as Punyunpkil, was not far behind Portland as the first settlement in Victoria.

The earliest known record of Port Fairy was made on the morning of 25 April 1810 when the cutter, *The Fairy*, captained by sealer James Wishart, sailed into the bay on which the present town is situated. Even though Wishart first saw the area under an equinoctial gale, it gave a favourable impression and his fancy suggested that the bay was worthy of a name as sentimental as that of his craft. He passed the shallow waters of the entrance and found the mouth of the River Moyne, called Gnarn Kolak by the natives. He sailed up the Moyne to where today Cox Street meets the river.

There was an abundance of seals and whales around Port Fairy and no doubt this attracted the first visitors to the bay. For twenty years the harbour was used by bay whalers who built huts along the river and foreshore for their six months' sojourn during the whaling season. A whaling station was established by Captain Jonathan Griffith on the island in the bay which now bears his name. Captain Griffith not only erected a residence on the island but had try works for the rendering down of the schools of whales which were captured in these waters. The Griffiths, father and son, and brothers John and Charles Mills, combined farming with their whaling operations, and appeared to be having success in the operation of the dual industries.

The last whale was caught off Port Fairy in 1848 but occasionally residents have seen whales out at sea.

Port Fairy was originally a temporary base, the whalers returning to Van Diemen's Land, where permanent settlement was made, every year.

This pattern changed after a few years and seamen such as Griffith, John and Charles Mills and Alexander Campbell began to treat Port Fairy as the more permanent home. Land was cultivated and more substantial housing erected.

Sheep were brought across the straits from Tasmania, despite the fact that the Government of New South Wales did not recognise any land rights in this remote section of the Colony.

By 1839 the population was large enough for Mr John Cox to open a store near the present corner of Cox and Gipps Streets. His store, located on the river bank amongst the she-oaks and wattles, was purchased by William Rutledge in 1843. However, this early enterprise was an isolated case and nothing appears of a formal village until the 1840s. One

'Merrijig Inn', on the corner of
Gipps and Campbell Streets, was
described in the *Portland Gazette* of
3 November 1844 as the older of Belfast's
'first class' hotels. It was probably built
in 1841 or 1842. Originally much larger
with a two-storied building along
Campbell Street, this inn was the first
meeting place (1856) of the Borough
Council and the magistrates also sat here
before the Court House was built.

Not only a tourist resort, Port
Fairy also houses a fishing fleet.
Lobster getting is an important industry
and here the pots are still manufactured
in the traditional method with cane
and wire.

Right
Port Fairy is mainly a tourist resort
for the western districts. It has a safe
harbour which was one of the attributes
early recognised by the whalers and
sealers who first settled in this district.

can only assume that Port Fairy was a shanty town, with temporary structures built of pisé, bark and timber resembling the first settlement at Sydney Cove where building materials were difficult to procure.

In September 1835 Lieutenant-Surveyor Wedge had visited Portland and Port Fairy and reported on the character and capacity of the harbours as well as the appearance of the country along the south-western coastline. This report, and private advices received from sea captains who had visited Port Fairy, that the soil in the area was exceptionally rich, soon reached Sydney. As a consequence the New South Wales solicitor James Atkinson, and William Rutledge, each obtained grants of 5,120 acres in 1839. This land was granted under the 'Special Survey' system adopted by the New South Wales Parliament to encourage settlement in remote areas of the colony. The grants were made without the knowledge of the then residents of the port.

Governor La Trobe at Port Phillip protested most strongly in correspondence to the central authorities against the allocation of so large an area to a single individual but Atkinson appears to have had more influence and won. Belfast, as Atkinson named the township, was bodily handed over at £1 an acre, an act which was to strangle the progress of the town as Atkinson did not sell but leased the land. This had far-reaching effects on the western districts of Victoria.

Atkinson was resolved to make quick profit through the subdivision of the estate. His grant extended from the mouth of the River Moyne and included virtually all the area upon which the present town of Port Fairy stands. He divided it into small leaseholds in a roughly gridiron pattern which was distorted by the river. This planned town was to house a population of over 200 people. After the land was subdivided a scheme of assisted immigration from Sydney, Van Diemen's Land and England was put into action. The scheme attracted many hundreds of settlers to the area, which was known as the 'Portland Bay Settlement'.

In 1844–46 cultivation advanced considerably. The farmers introduced by Atkinson settled on lands such as Duck Holes, The Black Swamp and Yates Hill and in 1843 Alexander Struth built the windmill which stood in the town at the end of Gipps Street. The mill itself was brought over from Sydney by Captain Grant in the brig *Socrates*. In 1847 it was purchased by William Rutledge & Co. and it continued to stand for many years.

Direct shipments of wool, gold and tallow were regularly dispatched from Port Fairy

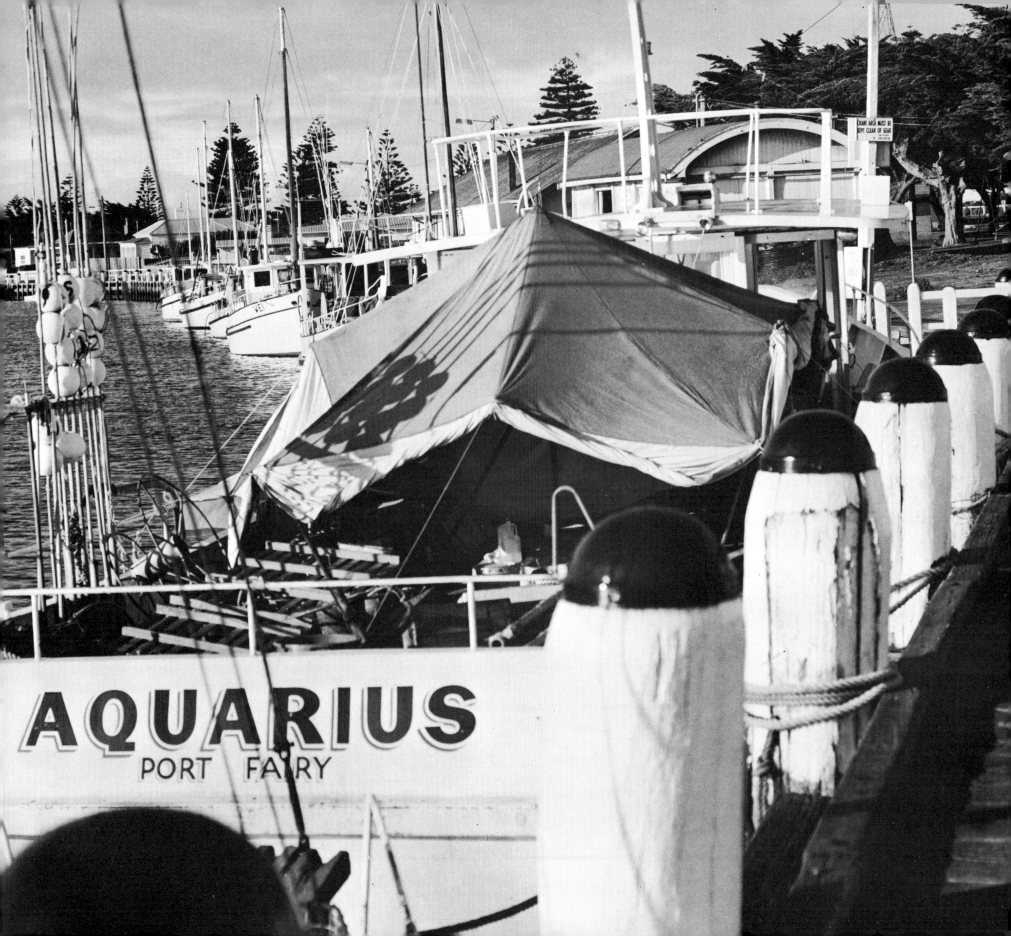

The milestone from Belfast to Yambuk reminds one of the town's original name.

The Court House in Gipps Street, an impressive classical building, was constructed in 1859 with additions in 1869. The interior still retains its fine woodwork almost in original condition.

between the sixties and seventies and for better lightering facilities Rutledge & Co. imported from England, in sections, a large iron, flat-bottomed lighter at the cost of £3,000. In putting it together, the worker fitted the plates incorrectly and had to take her to pieces again. It was not altogether an accident, according to some reports, as it lengthened the well-paid wages of the period. The lighter's maiden voyage nearly cost the lives of the four men who took her out on the river. A big roller caught her on the bar and twirled her around violently, flinging men into the sea. The lighter was finally a failure, as the broad beam prevented her sailing against the currents and seas at the mouth of the river.

Agriculture and grazing were flourishing by the 1850s and the sea trade between Hobart and Port Fairy was second only to Sydney. By 1850 the population of Port Fairy was half of the 400 at Portland, the earlier settlement to the west which was established in 1834 by Edward Henty. Port Fairy flourished and provided the early western districts' settlers with provisions. The gold rushes of the fifties did not drain away Port Fairy's population. In fact Port Fairy benefited from the boom by supplying the diggings with agricultural products. Portland, too, gained as it was the port of entry for many of the diggers and here they equipped themselves for the fields. To a certain extent Port Fairy reaped the shadow benefits.

In the 1861 census the population of Port Fairy was 2,300 and that of Portland 2,800. In 1862 the disastrous crash of William Rutledge & Co. occurred. This firm, with Port Fairy as its administrative headquarters, had activities stretching over the entire country. Much building had taken place prior to the crash, and it is to this period that the major buildings of Port Fairy belong.

In 1885 the great land sale in Port Fairy took place and most of the leaseholds of the town became freeholds. On 17 May 1887 Sir Henry Lock officially proclaimed the alteration of the town's name from Belfast to Port Fairy in the *Government Gazette*. This was the year of Queen Victoria's jubilee and Port Fairy joined in the universal congratulations to Her Majesty. High holiday was proclaimed on 21 June when a procession, marshalled by Commander Alexander Cameron on a wild white charger, with the brass band playing the National Anthem, marched to the Agricultural Society's grounds where a public feast was held, sports organised and the Jubilee medals presented to every child born in Port Fairy during Jubilee Year.

The main interest of the town lies between William Street to the west and the river to the east (with the bay beyond), between Campbell and Regent Streets. It is worth mentioning

Left
Not to be dismissed is this Gothic
holiday cottage with crisp and
incredibly complex valance and barge
boards carved in a vigorous manner.
These contrast with the heavy bluestone
walls. This cottage is an excellent
example of the 'cottage orné', which
appeared at the height of the nineteenth
century and appeared in many copy
books from which this example
was no doubt taken.

Above
Around Port Fairy are simple
Georgian cottages. Elementary in their
composition, they usually comprise a
central door with windows on either side
and the whole rectangular composition
is balanced by chimneys.

Left
Early Victorian architecture has
much opulence especially in the
detailing of barge boards and valances.
The verandah on this house has a
nautical flair.

This Georgian cottage is constructed from bluestone and its naval appearance is suggested by the white-trimmed windows and doors.

Right
The foundation stone of St John's Church was laid on 16 October 1854 and the architect was Nathaniel Billing. The Church is constructed from bluestone which gives it a sombre appearance. The tower is recent and was completed in 1959, designed by architect Rolf Crawley.

Over left & right
There is a feeling of south-west England in much of the architecture in Port Fairy, perhaps due to the white-washed stone work or the irregular shapes of many of its buildings.

some of the buildings in this area. There is the old Bank of Australasia (now the A.N.Z.) on the corner of Cox and Sackville Streets, designed by Nathaniel Billing and built in 1857; the Court House in Gipps Street, erected between 1859–60, with additions in 1869 and 1873 in keeping with the Palladian style. The Court is large for the size of Port Fairy, but was designed to cope with sessions of the Supreme Court as well as local country matters. Before 1859 court hearings were held at the local 'Merrijig Inn', a building from the earlier times.

There is 'Seacombe House' on the corner of Sackville and Cox Streets. This was originally built as the 'Stag Hotel' by Captain John Sanders in 1847. It continued as a hotel until 1888 and during its hey-day was the centre of the town's festivities. Dinners and dances were held in the upstairs ballroom and 'Promenade Concerts' were given nightly by such 'Unprecedented Attractions' as the Weder family and the 'Ethiopian Serenaders' whose musical instruments consisted of bones, banjo and concertina.

At 40 Gipps Street can be seen the house of one of the town's first settlers, Captain John Mills, who lived in this cottage during his term of office as Harbour Master from 1852–71. The materials, other than the stone, are supposed to have been brought from Van Diemen's land.

At number 8 Cox Street is 'Emoh', erected in 1844, William Rutledge's town house. St John's Church is not far away. It was designed by Nathaniel Billing and erected by local stone masons in 1856.

At the mouth of the river, opposite Griffiths Island, is Battery Hill and the fort. The lookout and flagstaff have been there since the early days of the settlement but the fort was a later addition. The guns, replacing older models, were installed in 1885. Firing these guns was an expensive operation as the blast broke the windows in the Moyne Flour Mills across the river.

There is much to see in Victoria's second oldest settlement and any quick survey will take you around the interesting architecture which remains from this time. There is a flavour of the sea about many of the buildings, an architecture which is simple and basic in its form, and sometimes white-washed or bluestone walls with large white joints which give the naval character to the buildings. The Norfolk Island pines planted along many of the streets reinforce this naval atmosphere as does the lighthouse, which was part of the port improvements made on the advice of the British harbour engineer, Sir John Coode, in 1902.

Today Port Fairy depends upon tourism—it is a holiday area for the western districts as well as a thriving fishing port.

152

HEARN'S HOTEL.
MELBOURNE
BITTER
Victoria
Bitter
RESTAURANT
SUNDAY
MEALS

Burra

South Australia

Where the ground was soft along the river banks, the early miners burrowed to form shelters. These correspond with the most primitive dwellings found at Matmata in Tunisia and Guadix in Spain where similar troglodyte communities exist.

Right
This troglodyte is more sculptured in its appearance than the former. Whole communities existed in the Burra region before the big flood of 1856 when a great number of these dwellings were swept away. After this flood the communities did not return to their former dwellings but continued to take refuge in the town.

Among the earliest-known dwelling places which man has devised, certainly the simplest and the most economical, are cave or earth dwellings. These dwellings are referred to as troglodytes and communities have been discovered in such diverse areas as China, Turkey, Italy and Tunisia. Where the earth was soft, the ground was moulded by primitive communities into a network of tunnels and chambers. At Guadix, in Spain, the inhabitants hollowed out additions to their cave dwelling in the soft rock and added structures to the faces of the caves—white conical chimneys were built to ventilate the interiors and white stucco walls were added to define yard spaces. Similarly in Matmata, in Tunisia, the troglodytes take the form of large oval cavities in the ground resembling a moonscape; some of the holes are 200 feet in diameter and about thirty feet deep and in these neighbourhoods as many as 100 people live.

Along the banks of the Burra Creek a similar troglodyte community was established with a population of nearly 2,000 persons. It was the first such community in Australia and, except for some small examples such as Coober Pedy, the only one of its kind in Australia.

South Australia was the last of the States to be settled but the first to have mining. Other States had prospectors—but serious mining first commenced after small samples of copper and other minerals were discovered around the Adelaide Hills. 'Coppermania' was the genuine predecessor to 'gold fever' and it ran through the newly-formed State with equal fervour.

The credit for mineral exploration in South Australia goes to Professor Johannes Mengé, a migrant from Germany, and an enthusiastic mineralogist. The Professor believed that the hills around Adelaide held much promise of minerals, especially gold and copper. Mengé found his minerals but was beaten to a positive claim by two Cornish miners who discovered an outcrop of silver and lead at Glen Osmond. Together with Professor Mengé they started one of the first mines in South Australia.

In 1842 the most northern town in South Australia was Gawler. Beyond that the land was unsurveyed and unexplored. As was the practice in many parts of Australia, this land had a sprinkling of illegal shepherds. In the far north, two shepherds named William Streair and Thomas Pickett found malachite and azurite. The shepherds lived seven miles apart and their discoveries were made in the same month of 1845 on the same range of hills. Both shepherds traded the locations to mining groups in Adelaide.

156

The town of Kooringa in 1848. A row of miners' cottages can be seen in the mid-foreground. It is interesting to see that the artist included natives in idyllic poses to romanticise the scenery.

A view of the Burra Burra Mine, 1848, showing the surface operation. The treeless hills with scattered miners' huts can be seen.

Right
The Market Square at Kooringa is a fine civic space around a bandstand. It has an extraordinarily-shaped roof complete with weathercock and the whole is constructed of cast iron pilasters and elements. The architecture of the town is unified by crisp white-painted heads, sills and quoins which contrast with the stone walls.

The dilemma was apparent when Governor Grey was presented with two separate applications, one from a group of settlers who were later to call themselves the South Australian Mining Association (nicknamed by the locals as the 'Snobs') and the other the Princess Royal Mining Association (the 'Nobs'). Control of the two outcrops of copper could not be obtained without a special survey, and this was difficult and cumbersome. Governor Grey insisted that the copper claim be made in one application. The claim was roughly a parallelogram in shape, eight miles long and four miles wide. Grey also insisted that the purchase price of £20,000 for the claim be paid in gold and that either company had three weeks to effect settlement.

In such a situation the Nobs and Snobs had little alternative but to unite. On purchase the Nobs and Snobs agreed to divide the area and lots were drawn for the two sections. The Snobs drew section one on the north containing Pickett's lode, later to become the Burra-Burra Mine, and the Nobs drew the southern section, the Princess Royal Mine, containing Streair's lode.

In September 1845 the Snobs opened the South Australian Mining Association and engaged ten Cornish miners plus a Cornishman, Captain Thomas Roberts, as mining overseer. The find at Pickett's lode was a bonanza and the company quickly realised the riches in store.

The Nobs were less fortunate. The mine soon petered out leaving the shareholders with 10,000 acres of good grazing land which was sold in 1851 as a sheep station. On the site chosen for the Princess Royal township a homestead bearing the same name was built in 1864.

The town of Burra grew up with the mine, a town built by the Cornish miners with climate or geography being the only elements affecting its architecture. The miners were mainly from St Just and Redruth and they selected the Burra Creek for their home sites. Up and down the creek bank houses were dug from the soft clay. In the heyday of the mines two thousand people burrowed out their houses and lived comfortably in these conditions.

One newspaper reported:
Upon arrival at the town the miners first job was to dig himself a home—and who better than a miner to do this? Passage ways connected each of the three or four rooms of the dugout and sleeping recesses were dug into the walls. Along the front of the home there was a shingled verandah with windows. Inside the rooms were white washed, or papered . . .

Burra was essentially a town created by people from Cornwall who translated their indigenous architecture directly into the Australian landscape with little variation. This view of small, compact cottages could be in Cornwall or some southern English town. Each cottage is expressed as an individual unit and the builder had sufficient sensitivity to stack the architecture up the hill in a satisfying way.

The gaol at Redruth was designed by the Colonial Architect and was ready for occupation in September 1856. It continued to operate until 1894 when it was converted to a girls' reformatory which it remained until the 1920s. The buildings are now in ruin.

Right
Paxton Square, named after William Paxton, a director and share-holder of the Burra Mines. The Square is unique and contains thirty-three cottages, originally of two rooms each. They were built by Cornish masons for the miners brought out in 1856 to work the deeper levels of mines. After the mines were closed the cottages were purchased by the Honourable John Lewis and left in trust to house the 'aged, poor and needy'.

In the floods of the 1850s hundreds of homes along the creek were washed away or flooded never to be rebuilt—now only two remain. The Burra Mine had problems when water was struck at a depth of one hundred feet. Keeping the mine dry was a constant worry and in 1851 the directors resolved to buy a powerful pumping engine from England. This 250 horse power engine was dragged by jinker from Adelaide and the latter remains there today.

Towns around the mine grew up from 1846. Kooringa was established by the Australian Mining Association to house miners. Other towns followed. Redruth was laid out by the Government in 1847 in order to combat the monopolistic aims of the mining company who had decided not to grant any freehold titles for blocks or buildings. Redruth was located half a mile from Kooringa and bordered the Mining Association property, which created an area of barren waste between the two towns.

Other towns, Aberdeen and New Aberdeen, were sited along the same border line but the mining proprietors fenced out the new towns and for twenty years would not allow a direct road for through traffic between the two. Today the remains of all these towns are lumped under the one title of Burra. A small distinction exists between Burra and Kooringa and Redruth as these remain today as Burra North. The half mile space which separated the towns is still a no-man's-land.

Burra flourished until 1877 when the mine eventually closed. It slowly became a forgotten frontier town.

The character of Burra is distinctively Cornish. The permanent buildings, other than the troglodytes, appear as transplanted pieces of Cornish architecture. Little rows of cottages stack gently up the hill slope, their skyline punctuated with chimneys, their front windows shaded by verandahs—the only concession to the Australian climate. The mines themselves were constructed in the Cornish tradition as robust forms with stone arches and lintels built for eternity and now fighting for their survival against the elements.

Ventilation stacks dot the horizon providing fresh air for the labyrinth mines. Pump houses give interesting silhouettes against the landscape.

In the main town of Burra there still exists the old market square of Kooringa with its hotels and shops shaded by wide verandahs. The plan is irregular and not at all typical of the usual mining town with its customary straight streets with buildings either side, rather it depends for its townscape on its irregularity and is therefore more reminiscent of villages in Cornwall.

There are many buildings of architectural merit within the town. Already mentioned are the Cornish-type cottages at Paxton Square, and these can be contrasted with the cottages at Redruth which are verandahless and more vernacular Cornish than Australian. There is the gaol, completed in 1856 and closed in 1894, the first gaol erected in South Australia outside the Adelaide area. There are other buildings, displaying a restrained, Victorian character, which complete the town: the Old Telegraph Office at Kooringa, the Burra Public School with its great rose window which was erected in 1877, the year the mine closed. The school was built to hold 800 children, and with land cost nearly £7,000.

There are the churches—St Joseph's Roman Catholic Church and St Mary's Church of England, both stone buildings. The Cornish people were strongly Methodist and the Redruth Methodist Church has fine detail within an almost simplistic architecture.

Around the township the hills are bare of trees and long grass waves in the wind. Scattered on this landscape are the gaunt shapes of the mines. There is a lonely feeling about Burra, perhaps caused by the lack of trees. In the town the Victorian Rotunda gives evidence of the more cheerful days when the mine was booming, there was plenty of work, and women were raffled in the local pubs.

Left & right
Mine ruins in the Burra area.

Mintaro

South Australia

The 'Mintaro Hotel' is an important visual element in the streetscape of Mintaro. Situated on the corner of the two main streets in the town it turns the corner successfully by extending the verandahs on both façades.

Right
At one time Mintaro was a thriving 'bullocky' stop over for the ore trains from the Burra Mines. The town supported much industry including hotels and boarding houses and here is the remains of a building locally called 'the mill'.

Some towns were established as dormitories for miners, some as markets for cattle. Others were established as resting places along the pioneering bullock trails. Such a town is Mintaro.

The Burra mines had been established in September 1845, 100 miles from Adelaide. In order to get to Burra a long and tedious journey, usually by bullock dray, was involved. The road from Adelaide to Gawler was reasonably direct, but north of Gawler the road was called 'Gluepot Road'—'a quagmire in winter and a torment of dust in the summer'.

The road north to Burra was established by bullockies who made their own roads, their own creek crossings, and their own camp sites, generally achieved with a native cunning and ingenuity which our sophisticated society would consider impossible now.

The bullocky was a race apart. One observer's description of the bullocky and his wool load arriving in town gives a picture of the team:

. . . while strolling in the outskirts of the town, above a cloud of dust I saw approaching a huge lumbering mass, like a moving haystack, swaying from side to side and I heard the creaking of wheels in the distance, and a volley of strange oaths accompanied by the sharp crack of a whip. Presently the horns of a pair of monstrous bullocks appeared, straining solemnly at their yokes; then another and another followed, until I counted five pairs of elephantine beasts, drawing a rude cart, composed of two high wheels and a platform without sides, upon which was packed and piled bales of wool full fourteen feet in height. Close to the near wheel stalked the driver, a tall, broad-shouldered, sunburnt, careworn man . . . In his hands he carried a whip, at least twenty feet long, with the thong of which, with perfect ease, he every now and then laid into his leaders, accompanying each stroke with a tremendous oath.

Ten miles of travel per day was a good rate for a bullock team. Stops were made on the way and generally the day's start was made at sunrise and ended at sunset.

At night the bullocks were turned out to feed. Bells were attached to the bullocks in open country so that they could be easily found. At dawn the bullocky would get up and follow the tracks of his animals into the bush, herd them together and yoke them for their hard day's work ahead.

The bullockies opened up the roads to the mines and at each night's stop there was soon a collection of inns and shops, servicing the bullockies' needs. The establishment of towns like Mintaro can be compared with today's towns which cater for truck drivers who congregate together to swap yarns and tales at their favourite cafe or roadside inn.

Mintaro is composed, for the most part, of vernacular stone cottages with galvanised roofs some of which have verandahs formed by the extension of the main roof. Other verandahs are formed by a separate skillion as shown in this cottage. The common space formed by the intersection of the various road systems creates a civic space in Mintaro.

Right
The streets in Mintaro are lined with ancient trees. Their intricate root systems form part of the streetscape. They are serpentine and restless and appear to writhe over the pavement.

The bullock path from Burra to Adelaide soon became the major highway north. Along this road the bullockies dragged the ore from the Burra mines to be loaded on to the ships in the Port of Adelaide for shipping to Wales for smelting. The need for a more economic system of production which involved less transport was realised and in 1849 the South Australian Mining Company gave a lease to the English and Australian Copper Company to bring out Welsh smelters to treat the ore at the mine site. Alternate sites were also inspected for port facilities as Adelaide was considered too distant. Port Wakefield was subsequently established in Gulf St Vincent.

A sixty-mile road from the Burra mines to Port Wakefield was surveyed and staked out. Officially it was gazetted as the Great Western Road but the word 'great' existed in name only. The road proved more of a problem than the North Road, especially for bullock drays, and the company turned to mule trains in order to combat the bad conditions.

In 1853 the barque *Malacca* arrived in Port Wakefield with its first load of mules. Only seventy of the 180 mules from Spain had survived the journey. In April another two hundred arrived and by degrees a working team of 400 mules was built up. During the winter months the mules carried ore in panniers from the mine and a return load of Newcastle coal to the smelters.

Along the Great Western Road, and to mark each day's rest, the following towns grew— Mintaro, Auburn, Watervale, Balaklava, Leasingham, Bowmans and Whitwanta. Mintaro survives better than most of the other towns and expresses the atmosphere of the 'bullocky' days. The buildings are all vernacular and there are no high style architectural examples— just a pub, a few shops, and the remains of hostelries and inns which catered for the bullock teams and travellers.

As you come into the town from Burra, the spatial experience of Mintaro is good. On the right is the police house and in the distance can be seen two houses framing the entry to the town proper. Mintaro is built as a triangular shaped plan. At one angle is the pub, at another the churches and on the third are ruins. One arm of the triangle leads to Port Wakefield, the other to the slate quarry.

The 'Mintaro Hotel' is a white-painted single-storey structure surrounded by verandahs. From the urbanscape point of view it makes a distinct contribution to the triangular site, especially as the hotel verandah gives ever changing vistas as you walk around. There is

Formerly a shop, this building has fallen into ruin for lack of attention. The construction of the façade can be seen in layered slate forming the basic carcass of the wall. Slate voussoirs form the circular headed openings.

Far right
The civic buildings such as the Post Office and banks were grouped together in Mintaro. The Post Office retains a Victorian restraint due to the simple materials used in its construction. In the cottages in the background the influence of Cornish architecture can be evidenced in the steepness of the roof and the slenderness of the chimney details. The skyline of Mintaro was once punctuated by such chimneys.

The final visual quality of towns depends upon the approaches which, in the case of Mintaro, are excellent. There is an air of expectancy created by the formalised planting of Eucalyptus trees.

Right
Standing slightly separate from the town are the churches built for congregations which no longer exist. The architecture is simple and noble as only the simplest geometric forms are used.

nothing pretentious about this building, no frills, no slick architectural trappings and the lack of these gives this it dignity.

The same can be said for the shops and houses in the main street. Most of the public buildings, such as the Post Office, are constructed from local slate with wide joints, the quoins rendered or picked out in white. The eaves, brackets and other elements of architectural definition such as window heads and sills are also painted. The chimneys and the scale of many of the houses suggest a Cornish architecture. This is natural as many of these buildings were constructed by Cornish miners who changed their native architecture little for the Australian scene. Along one street are the ruins of an old mill house and store. This could represent a gaunt scene, yet there is enormous warmth in the stone walls with the dressed stone quoins to dispel this feeling. There are ruins of other buildings around—shops and houses as well as buildings of indeterminate use.

Many of these buildings retain their fine slate walls constructed as dry walls. In Mintaro today slate is being quarried for commercial purposes.

Surveying the scene are the two churches; the Roman Catholic and the Methodist. The latter is a magnificent set of buildings with rectory, church hall and church proper in a complex which forms a rough courtyard space. They are constructed in freestone in a simple neo-Gothic style. The rectory has little ornament—only the gable which has a garden Gothic expression over the front door. The rest of the buildings are simple, with ornaments being constrained to a few string and head courses. Throughout the entire town the landscape prevails. The old fig trees grow with giant knotted bases from which run artery systems of roots. Silver-trunked gum trees give a constant rhythm throughout the town and finally march off steadily along the road out of Mintaro.

Strathalbyn

South Australia

A view of Strathalbyn. Mitchell Library Collection, date unknown. In the foreground are the common areas along the Angas River. A cricket game is in progress and the spectators are sitting on logs. The composition of the town could be an idealised form of English village rather than an Australian country town.

Right
The Presbyterian Church of Strathalbyn dates back to the beginnings of the town. The grantees laid out the town reserving large areas along the river for recreation as well as a site in the centre of the town for the church. An acre of ground was also set aside for a cemetery. The church is modelled on a baronial interpretation of the Gothic and is beautifully sited.

The town of Strathalbyn formed part of the Angas Special Survey and is laid out on a section of land granted to Dr William Rankine and James Dawson in 1841.

The grantees laid out the town in a broad and liberal manner, reserving a large area on either side of the River Angas for recreation purposes, as well as a site for a Presbyterian Church and a cemetery.

Strathalbyn, or 'The White Valley', was named by Dr Rankine. Very soon the region was attracting a large farming and pastoral population, particularly families of Scottish origin. It was said in Adelaide that 'all roads lead to Strathalbyn'.

A general store was established which attracted other trade, a bridge was constructed over the Angas and was called, in good Scottish tradition, St Andrew's Bridge. It was a large timber structure with a central timber arch. Another bridge was soon put across and was called Gal-Col-Hoop Bridge after the builders, Gallan, Colman and Hooper. There were no events which single out Strathalbyn as a town of special history—perhaps its consistent growth caused by pastoral activities, changed only by a small amount of mining towards the end of the century, is the cause of this.

A district Council, which embraced the town and district for many miles around, was formed and in 1868 the town became incorporated. In the early 1870s many of the young men from the south areas of Strathalbyn went north as it was opened for settlement, and also to the Wimmera District of Victoria where there was a right of selection before survey, on easy interest-free terms of payments, extending over twenty years. The result of all this was that land in the Strathalbyn district gradually became amalgamated into large holdings.

In 1903 many of these large estates were broken up and subdivided into smaller farms.

This pleased the Strathalbyn people immensely, and accordingly E. H. Tucker J.P., the Mayor, on the evening of the auction sale of the 'Merchant Estate', one of the large land holdings, gave a reunion banquet at the 'Tennines Hotel', which all the then living ex-mayors, ministers of the crown and old residents, together with leading local identities, attended. Speeches were made and toasts given to the Premier and Ministry of South Australia on its magnificent attitude in purchasing the 'Merchant Estate' for the people.

The town is picturesquely sited along the Angas River, giving a civic dimension which most country towns in Australia lack. From the tree-shaded river with its splashing waterfowl the spires of the town churches can be seen. The whole townscape has an idyllic

The ruins of this shed have a geometry and an architectural honesty which always appeal.

Right
The 'Argus House' is one of many Victorian commercial buildings within the town. The cantilevered verandah gives a delicate feeling to the façade which is further accented by the extremely slender first floor columns. The ground floor consists of shop front and doorway for shopkeepers' residence.

quality reminiscent of many villages in England. The buildings also have a quality and permanence which reflects the stable nature of the early Presbyterian settlers.

Agricultural communities in Australia have, in some places, followed the 'central place' theory, especially where the land was of consistent contour and of reasonably equal fertility. Central places may be defined as clusters or agglomerations of functions within a limited geographical area which provide services throughout a much wider area.

The first concept of central place is a population threshold and a town does not exist unless there is sufficient demand within a rural area for its presence. The second notion is of the range of goods with hierarchical orders of towns depending upon goods and services offered. These roughly correspond with hamlets, villages, towns, cities and metropolises.

A country region can be composed of many small towns providing essential district services. Within the region there is a large town which assumes greater significance and is the centre of government and church, and similarly within a state or larger region there is usually a town of city proportions affording goods and services of still greater order. These orders of hierarchy are called first, second and third orders and the boundaries form themselves into a hexagon pattern of territorial division. Obviously this bee-hive like pattern distorts with geographical features and unnatural or political circumstances.

Strathalbyn represents a town of the higher order of development because of the range of services it affords and its importance as an educational, ecclesiastical and political centre, and the town form indicates this.

There are many fine stone buildings in Strathalbyn of a restrained Victorian architectural style. The Savings Bank of South Australia has rusticated stone work with rendered and pointed window reveals and arches. The Post Office bears the same Victorian overtone with pedimented gables and symmetry achieved in most of the façade patterns. Argus House, by contrast to the Post Office and Savings Bank, has a lighter quality to the façade with cantilevered awning.

The main shopping centre has a variety of commercial buildings, generally single-storey constructions with verandahs. There is more feeling of Art Nouveau decoration in the iron work in the verandah spandrels than in many other towns, more of the sensuous and tendril form of ornament which characterises this period. One of the more restrained and almost classical examples of Victorian commercial architecture is seen in the National Bank which has

symmetrical façades and was constructed of random rubble with rendered quoins and string courses. The eaves have a stub joist and this gives a gentle decoration to the façade. Along the main entrance façade an iron picket fence completes the urban vocabulary.

Around the town centre the park is always present, coupled with the Angas River which flows through the town. On an island in the middle of the river a pavilion has been built, a typical band rotunda where much of the social life of the town once existed. It was in this park that the festivities took place for visiting Royalty, and it is here that the townspeople today enjoy the quiet of Strathalbyn. Black swans have now found refuge in the park. Standing within the trees, the silhouette of the town can be appreciated with its towers and chimneys expressing the full flood of prosperity.

The architecture of the Victorian commercial buildings in Strathalbyn is restrained and almost echoes the simplicity of the Georgian which is concerned with the balance between solid and void. Here the same kind of essay is involved together with the textural quality of walls where coursed rubble walls contrast with rendered quoins. The building is the National Bank of Australasia.

Right
The use of stone with dressed quoins is typical of many structures in Strathalbyn. The street pattern is broken up by over-hanging two-storied verandahs and diverse forms of single-storied verandahs. Each contribute to the character and the intrigue of the town.

Verandahs form the character of the shops surrounding the park.

Right
The lightness and delicacy of the console brackets of these verandah posts is unusual for Victorian cast iron patterns. There is a freshness in the approach here, almost the sinuous line predicting Art Nouveau.

Far right
Central Park in Strathalbyn. The character and dignity of the town depends upon the parklands bordering the Angas River.

Goolwa

South Australia

The railway superintendent's house. Photograph 1869. Note the gazebo in the garden which was once a feature of many Victorian gardens.

Right
The remains of the railway superintendent's house.

In February 1830 Captain Charles Sturt and his party reached the mouth of the River Murray having travelled the inland waterways of the Murrumbidgee and Murray Rivers in a whale boat. To Sturt the site was disappointing—instead of a noble harbour with a navigable entrance he found a sand bar, not a fitting climax for the greatest river in Australia.

Sturt's reports on the lands along the Murray were promising and prompted the Government to found settlements along the river.

Colonel William Light was given instructions by the Government to inspect the areas around the Murray delta as the site for a possible port and Sturt again inspected the mouth of the Murray in 1838 and confirmed his original opinion.

Governor Gawler was interested in the Murray River and its potential. He had explored the river system himself as far as the present town of Morgan and had realised that the river was of major importance as a traffic route for the wool and wheat of the interior.

Gawler saw the potential of nearby Victor Harbour as a port and envisaged a plan for utilising the river system. He saw the Murray River could be used for the major transport artery as far as Goolwa. From here goods could be taken across land by train or canal to Victor Harbour where they could be lightered on to ships. His plan was not realised and, hampered by economic conditions in the Colony, the scheme was abandoned.

Sir Henry Edward Fox Young, South Australia's fifth Governor, also explored the Murray system. His journey closely followed the plan of operation envisaged by Gawler. He persuaded the Government to offer a prize of £2,000 each for the owners of the first two steam boats to navigate the river from Goolwa to Wentworth.

Captain Francis Cadell had been working on the Australian coastal run and was determined to win. He had previously inspected the mouth of the Murray and was fascinated by the prospects of the adventure. He ordered his steamer, the *Lady Augusta*, from Chaume & Co., shipbuilders of Pyrmont, but in the meantime William Randell, son of a wealthy land owner and miller, also entered the contest with the *Mary Ann*. The contest between the two boats reads like *Three Men in a Boat* with mishaps and groundings, boats being tangled in trees or following each other up the wrong river arm. The race was won by the *Lady Augusta*, and the event was instrumental in opening up the Murray River system to traffic.

Goolwa was selected as the site for the River port terminal. The name, being aboriginal for elbow, aptly describes the bend of the river on which the town was founded.

A typical tramway cab which ran between Goolwa and Port Elliot, 1870.

Old Government stables built to house horses used on the tramcar. Photograph taken 1939.

Right
Goolwa in the 1880s. The *Waradgery*, the *Gem* and the *Ariel* in foreground.

Port Elliot instead of Victor Harbour was chosen as the ocean-going harbour.

It was decided to link Goolwa and Port Elliot by either a railway or canal system and surveys between the two were made in 1849 by R. T. Hill.

The former scheme was adopted. Rails, truck wheels and all railway equipment had to be imported from England. By 1851 work had commenced at Port Elliot. The rails were laid on timber bearers placed at right angles to the track without a continuous timber bearer. Only in places where wear was expected was the conventional continuous bearer used. Large stores were constructed at each terminal, and at Port Elliot a three-storied structure was built to receive the goods. This building lasted until 1896 when it was demolished.

On 18 May 1859 the project was complete. Wool was brought down the Murray River system by steamer, unloaded at Goolwa, transferred by rail to Port Elliot where it was unloaded on to lighters and taken by ship to overseas markets.

With the project complete people began moving into the area. Until this time there had been little activity in the grazing lands south of Adelaide. The gold rush in Victoria created a stimulus to the river trade, which provided the necessary transport for equipment and goods upstream to the goldfields. Flour mills were created to add more viability to the economy of the railway and so Goolwa prospered with both wheat and wool being processed there.

The town consisted of several ports: Town on the Goolwa, North Goolwa and Goolwa Extension. The first area to be surveyed was Town on the Goolwa in January 1840. Sections of the town were allocated by ballot in 1841 to holders of land in orders of ninety acres, composed of eighty country acres, eight acres in the town of Currency Creek, and two acres in Town on the Goolwa.

In *South Coast Story* J. C. Tolley says:

It is interesting to note that in this survey the blocks fronting the river were long and narrow, running from the water's edge and it has been suggested that they were laid out in a similar pattern to some English port areas where wharehouses had been provided to facilitate the receipt of cargo direct from the discharging ships. From this it seems that as early as 1840 hopes were held for developing the trading possibilities of the Murray, which in fact did not materialize for some years.

The most suitable site for a wharf was found to be south of the surveyed Town on the Goolwa and accordingly another town was surveyed. This is the present town of Goolwa, surveyed by Richard Brooking, and consisted of twenty-one quarter-acre blocks. These were

This sandstone residence, which fronts the main street, was built when Goolwa was a thriving river port.

Above right
The remains of Goolwa's once-vital river wharf.

Below right
The main street of Goolwa, once a bustling thoroughfare, now experiences a slower pace. The buildings have a consistent vernacular quality which gives the town an urban dignity.

sold at auction in 1853 and realised an average price of £20.

The wharf was constructed in 1852, government buildings quickly followed and the Post Office was erected in 1853. Buildings for commerce and trading were erected, pubs, hotels and boarding houses all made Goolwa a busy and bursting town. A scene of the activity in Goolwa and Victor Harbour:

. . . about 1,200 bales of wool were sent between Goolwa and Victor Harbour during the last season. At the present time two or three new steamers for the river trade are being built at Goolwa and as many repairing. During the height of the season the river presents a very busy sight, and only a few weeks ago there were fourteen or sixteen steamers and as many barges lying along the banks.

Goolwa became a ship-building centre for the Murray steamers. The Goolwa ironworks were established in 1846 but ships were not constructed there for a further three years. From 1860 onwards barges were built to cater for the expanding river traffic.

Between 1902–12 some shipbuilding took place, but mostly the yards were involved in repair work. After 1912 most of the activity had ceased.

By the mid-1880s the volume of trade had begun to fall away as a result of the steam railway between Morgan, and later Murray Bridge, and Adelaide. The slow turn-round of vessels caused by the horse-drawn railway link between Goolwa and Victor Harbour also brought a decline in traffic to the port. Even though the method of operation was changed from horse-drawn trains to steam, from 1910 Goolwa began to decline as an industrial town until now its river boat days are a memory.

The railway system still plays an important part in the urbanscape of the town, the system of tracks from the early days can be traced down to Port Elliot. The buildings within the town itself express the hustle and commercial activity of former times, and many of these were constructed in stone for permanence. The details of these buildings have similarities of brick quoins, brick heads and window sills which give a sharp contrast and a crisp effect to the architecture both in colour and texture. Many of the buildings are verandahless, and therefore assume more austerity than other buildings in the State which are softened by verandahs, which create either dark recesses or the play of lace shadows cast by ironwork and verandah ornamentation.

Today Goolwa relies upon the tourist industry for its main economy, and visitors can meander through the old town and dream of river days that have passed.

184

York

Western Australia

Adjacent to the Post Office is the
Court House and Police Station.

Right
York is a busy agricultural town and
was the saving factor in the success of
the colonisation of Western Australia.
Before the discovery of the rich pastures of
the Avon Valley, Perth was almost
destined to starvation. York therefore has
historical association with the early
settlement, but little remains of
the architecture of this period.

The Avon Valley has often been referred to as Western Australia's reprieve. The Swan River
Colony was proclaimed by Captain James Stirling R.N. on 18 June 1829 on the banks of the
Swan River. This early settlement was constantly without sufficient food and the continual
arrival of colonists was an embarrassment to Stirling. The limits of colonisation were confined
to the coastal regions and there was little exploration of the eastern territories beyond the
mountain range.

The first exploration of the eastern region was made by Robert Dale in July 1830. His
instructions, issued by Stirling, were to find suitable grazing or agricultural lands. Over the
Darling Ranges suitable land was discovered. To verify the reports, Captain Stirling and a
group of colonists explored the area again in October of the same year and confirmed Dale's
finding. The river flowing in the plain was called the Avon and the area which, with some
stretch of the imagination resembled Yorkshire, was suitably named. Within a year of
discovery of the eastern plain settlers began moving into the area. The town of York was
gazetted and Beverley and Northam soon followed.

The settlement in the Avon Valley was successful and the valley was quickly filled with
sheep runs and pastoral settlement. The shepherds were the real pioneers as often the squatters
would stay in Perth, trusting their flock to their employees.

In York basic quarters were adopted; sometimes the shepherd huts were made from earth
pug and roofed by the reeds of the xanthorrhoea, a grass-tree.

The early primitive buildings would have resembled any other town in Australia during its
formative period. It was noted by H. W. Bunbury when he visited York in 1836 that 'the
town consisted of five houses, a barn and a barrack' and it is probable that these would have
been constructed by the simplest possible means from pisé or timber.

As the district attracted more settlers, the primitive buildings were gradually replaced by
ones of substance. But along the outskirts of the town today it is still possible to see early
buildings. Although they may not belong to the time of the first settlement, they still possess
the same qualities. The early buildings were rectangular-shaped, divided into four parts. In the
front were the bedrooms, in the back the sitting rooms. A kitchen in many cases was detached
because of the fear of fire and the unbearable heat in the summer months but, in many, the
kitchen was incorporated in one of the back rooms. When the early settlers built their farm
house, their hotel, inn, or shop, they knew the type in question and style—what remained to

186

The architect for the Post Office was
G. K. Poole and the building was
constructed from rough-cut stone
within a framework of brick quoins and
string courses. The building was
erected in 1895 and has many instances of
Art Nouveau architecture,
especially the segmental arch.

Right
The Town Hall in York was built
in 1911, situated at the southern end
of Avon Terrace and separate from the
main group of public buildings. It has a
strange architectural style quite mad for
its surroundings. Constructed in stucco
and brick, it has a flamboyant clock with
entablature. The fanlight to the main
entry is finely worked and relieves the
structure of its heavy quality.

be determined was size. The characteristics of the vernacular are therefore a lack of theatrical or intellectual overtones, or aesthetic pretensions; they are essentially forces working in harmony with the microclimate. The broad verandahs of the early houses in York are a fitting example of this quality.

The houses in York are unpretentious in their architecture, they fit in—they don't vie with one another, jostle for position or claim the deficiencies of the egomania of the inhabitants. They are content to take their place and play their own role within the street. Their materials were limited to brick, either rendered or painted, and timber. The shingle roofs of the houses were invariably hipped with a variable treatment of verandah, supported on slender columns, which reduced the scale of building to very human proportions.

The town prospered in the 1840s and an agricultural association for the sale and show of stock and wool was established. The road between York and Perth was difficult and sale yards and exhibition centres within York itself were built. In *Western Pioneers*, Jesse E. Hammond say:
In no other settlement in the colony were the people so closely together as in York between 1860 and 1880. This led to the opening of a number of business places, all of which flourished. A condition that led to the people of York living more comfortably, on the whole, than those of other districts, for they were less frequently obliged to go to Perth or Freemantle, and had more time to work on their farms.

Mrs Hammond tells us:
. . . the settlers of York were a happy and united band and did everything they could to assist each other and to attract other settlers and visitors to the district. They organized what was called "York Fair" which was held once a year and lasted for five days. The programme included horse racing, ploughing matches, and a number of evening entertainments. The York Fair became very popular, and hundreds of people went there from Perth, Freemantle and all neighbouring towns.

During the Fair accommodation was always scarce but its success was responsible for many people taking up land in and around York.

An early industry was sandalwood in which many of the settlers traded. Mrs Hammond mentions the settlers and this industry:
Some of them have told me how their wives cleared the bark off the sandalwood while they were carting it into Perth or Guildford. These good wives did much of that sort of work to assist their husbands but at the same time they never forgot that they were mothers and had other duties to perform.

The town of York has no plan of special interest. It looks well with the landscaped areas of

An affinity between the architecture and soil is expressed in this barn which almost appears to grow out of the earth. It was built in an age where vernacular models were well known and the builders had a native ability to interpret form.

On the outskirts of York buildings of a vernacular type remain which express the early days of the colony. The shapes of the architecture are simple and appear to hug the earth with low-scaled verandahs.

Right
A group of small cottages in York.

the river and from the surrounding hills it nestles amongst the trees. The main street is Avon Terrace along which the principal buildings of the town have been erected. By far the most bold is the Town Hall complex, a two-storied building constructed from carefully-laid brickwork with large surrounds of stuccoed pilasters and balustrading. It is a strange building —the large entrance seems out of place—almost as if the design was intended for the entrance of a railway station. The fanlight and doorway are delicately detailed and this contrasts with the massive corner pediment with clock tower.

There are the customary civic buildings—the Post Office, 1895, built from a honey-coloured stone and contrasted with red brick quoins, string courses and arches. It is a vigorous design and has Art Nouveau influences with the giant segmental arch entrance. The architect was G. K. Poole. Next to the Post Office is the Court House, a two-storey building without any windows on the ground floor. The ground floor matches the Post Office. Next to the Court House is the Police Station, a single-storied building which continues the same architectural theme.

In the town are many examples of good Victorian architecture: shops and banks; drapers; grocers; offices for solicitors, lawyers and barristers; and, like other Australian towns, the finest buildings are generally the Victorian hotels, at the end of Avon Terrace, with encircling verandahs of timber. In one there is the apparent influence of Art Nouveau in the segmental arches constructed from lattice which are repeated in a subtle manner in the windows of the ground floor. The hotel on the opposite corner reflects the same feeling in an earlier Victorian style. It has cast iron railings and balustrade to the verandah which cantilevers over the street.

York still remains a prosperous town and its considerable value is in the early role it played in the development of Western Australia. In addition it has many vernacular buildings which recall a struggling community of former days.

Inside the chapel of the Church of the Holy Trinity, constructed in 1858.

Right
Reminiscent of early English Church architecture, this church is built from a variety of shapes, styles and patterns and yet preserves an architectural whole and consistency. The square tower is stripped of ornament except for the brickwork which is accented by string courses. The Nave and the Chancel are simple gable forms punctuated by lancet windows.

Coolgardie

Western Australia

These hotels in Coolgardie form an important part of the streetscape. They are lofty and elegant in their proportions and do not suffer from their lack of cast iron. It appears as though they were always intended to have open timber lattice panels.

Over left
The Warden's Court is one of the finest buildings in the gold fields. It was designed by John H. Grainger, an officer of the department of public works, and was erected in 1898. The builder was John Philip and the building cost £10,825.

Over right
The old post office buildings stand next to the Warden's Court. These were constructed in 1896 and now house the police station and post office. The eastern section of the complex was originally designed as a single storey building, a second storey being added in 1898 as a residence for the postal inspector.

If you were to draw a straight line through Western Australia from Esperance Bay to the Ashburton River, it would roughly define a high ridge or the crest of a dome. From the ridge the land seems to stretch endlessly to the east across to the edges of the Great Victoria Desert. To the west and south lie the Indian Ocean and the Southern Ocean respectively.

Arthur Bayley and William Ford reported their find of this area on 17 September 1892: *There stood the reef about eight feet in length and five feet in width and height, of stained and white quartz in which the gold was visible from a distance in thin veinlets, strips or patches.*

Of the sample which Bayley brought back to the town, 554 ounces of gold were won— and the rush was on.

Little was known of this country in the early days. A track had been blazed in 1863 by H. M. Lefroy into the hinterland as far as the Gnarlbine Rocks and the Colgardagnamma holes. Over this same track came many thousands of prospectors. In the *Coolgardie Gold Fields* W. Nicholas warns:

You can't travel the Coolgardie goldfields without a big purse, as this item will make plain; and every thing else is in proportion, whether in labour or in goods. It costs a lot of money and time, and some hardship, to get there, and people will often say, if you grumble at the prices, they don't spend their days in the very outskirts of civilization and discomfort, and unmentioned risks, etc., without they make money.

Without an adequate supply of water, hardship and sickness went hand in hand. The less hardy fell victim as the *Gold Fields Courier* of 8 December 1894 says:

. . . low fever and other ailments incidental to the advent of summer are now prevalent on the goldfields. Every other camp or tent has its sick man, and in not a few, the empty bunk speaks as eloquently as does the silent sorrow. and sadness which hangs about the tent of some poor dead mate or chum who has passed in his checks; low fever sufferers are mostly young men, who know little or nothing of fever treatment— quite a number have died from sheer neglect—and the tents of the sick are occupied by men for the most part in straightened circumstances, and unable to pay for medical attendance and skilled nursing.

The Coolgardie goldfield extended for many miles and consisted mainly of auriferous gold. The first settlement was on and around the claims near Fly Flat and a town was formerly proclaimed on 25 August 1893. The earliest dwellings were constructed from 'hop-bush' (a type of scrub bush), on a small timber frame. The front door was usually bullock hide. Some of the more affluent buildings were constructed in iron.

A streetscape of Coolgardie showing the main street at the turn of the century.

Equipping Prospectors, Coolgardie. The want of water was always a problem and the water drums can be seen strapped to the camel on the left.

In *The Land of Gold* the early settlement can be pictured:

The main street, which is called after the lucky finder of the first gold in the neighbourhood, Bayley, is a very wide thoroughfare, and when the shops and stores on either side, at present constructed of corrugated iron, are rebuilt in brick and stone, as they undoubtedly will be some day, it will present a very imposing appearance. . . Still these stores, in their very newness, gave to my mind a certain amount of character to the street, and with the heaps of packing cases and goods in front of them, and their large name boards overhead, imparted an idea of "big business" which is quite in keeping with a rough though successful mining camp for such it is in reality. The dusty roadway crowded with teams, camel caravans, buggies, horsemen and bicyclists, made up quite an inspiring scene.

There is much to amuse in the description of the roaring mining towns. There was almost every variety of shop 'except fishmongers' and the early dwellings in the town combined a variety of activity. There were combination confectioner and hairdressers, restaurants and laundries—obviously the early proprietors of such establishments were not content to put all their eggs in one basket. The early prospectors complained of a lack of 'amusement', a need that was exaggerated by the extreme loneliness of the town situation. A traveller of that time complained that:

Coolgardie is not yet well off for amusements—a rough sort of hall is occasionally used for musical entertainments, and there are one or two fairly good clubs; but after dark the resources for helping one to while away the time are as yet not numerous, considering what a lot of money there is to be spent among the crowd in the town after working hours, with the result that the drinking saloons and billiard-rooms are doing a roaring trade. In fact the thirst which the now famous Coolgardie dust induces is making the fortunes of many a publican, and the daily takings at many a small bar sufficiently proving this, £60 to £70 being not an unusual average. The great drawback to this part of the colony, want of water . . .

As more gold was discovered so the town grew and the first stone buildings were erected. In the 1890s Coolgardie was linked to Perth by telegraph line. In March 1896 the railway line between Southern Cross and Northam was opened and by September of the same year it was extended to Kalgoorlie. The Coolgardie railway station was built in 1896, in a grand manner with central pavilion shaded by a verandah with symmetrical flanking masses.

Water was an ever-constant worry to the town and the Mines Water Supply Office was built in 1897 to cope with the problem.

198

This building was used until 1903.

The Chamber of Mines and Commerce (as well as the School of Mines), was built in 1899, a robust building of stone and brick, in classical construction, with octagonal tower surmounted by a high Victorian canopy and rails.

By far the most elegant building in Coolgardie is the Warden's Court, erected between June and October of 1898, on the north side of Bayley Street. The architect was John H. Grainger from the Public Works Department in Perth. The building is symmetrical about a three-storied central block constructed from dressed grounds. On the granite floor a series of semi-circular arches with rendered soffits forms a broad, shaded arcade. The second floor has elongated windows of strange proportions with alternating pedimented and segmental entablatures. The centre block is crowned by a large pediment with coats of arms contained within it. The building has the feeling of the gold rushes, and the contrasting painted mouldings and balustrades give vitality.

The old Post Office, built in 1896, now houses both the police department and the Post Office. The same architectural vocabulary of granite blocks with brick quoins, heads and architraves to windows, is used in this building. The Post Office, originally of one storey, is entirely built from stone. A second storey was added as a residence for the postmaster and this helped the proportions of the final product. The new Post Office building replaced an earlier structure designed with a stubby tower.

At the peak of its development, Coolgardie could boast twenty-three hotels, three breweries, several newspaper offices, a stock exchange and all the ingredients which make a flourishing town.

The stock exchange did brisk trading amongst the miners.

One of the principal features of Coolgardie, and one which struck me as being quite unique, was the evening "open call" Stock Exchange, which was held in the hall of the large building just erected by the London and Western Australian Exploration Company. I walked in by chance after dinner one evening without knowing what was going on, and was much surprised when I learnt that the rough unkept crowd of men I saw around me, most of whom did not look worth a shilling, were engaged in buying and selling shares in the various mines of the district, and that in this manner the market price of the stock was often made.

There was a state of feverish activity in those days. The news of a new find would rouse the expectations of the small prospector and diggers. Usually without waiting to verify

Camels formed a part of the transport system across the arid region of Western Australia. Here an early photograph shows a camel train outside the Mutual Stores, Bayley Street, Coolgardie, and the Horse Bazaar.

information about the finds, or even its exact whereabouts, they would be up and off. Sometimes the roads had the appearance of a wartime scene, with the whole population on the move. There are many tales told of the distances covered and the deprivation and the natural disappointments that awaited most.

The town of Coolgardie still bears the vigour and excitement of the gold rushes. Although the great populations have gone it is possible to imagine those days through the buildings which are grand and pompous, unashamed of their vulgarity.

The Railway Station at Coolgardie was constructed by the Wilkie Brothers, as part of a contract for 115 miles of railway between Southern Cross and Coolgardie. It was officially opened in 1896.

Right
Parts of Coolgardie which once incorporated a bustling commercial centre. Alongside these buildings were others forming a continuous street pattern. The building on the extreme right is now the R.S.L. Club.

Far right
On the outskirts of town, on the edge of the great desert, stands a Roman Catholic Presbytery and school.

Broome

Western Australia

Pearl luggers at Broome. The pearl industry has had a chequered career in recent years and much of the activity has been centred upon the harvesting of pearl shells for the cultured pearl industry. The main support of the industry in former times was buttons but, after the Second World War, this was eclipsed by the plastic industries.

Right
Broome might be called architecturally dull but to many it is an interesting essay of various vernacular types. The town is predominantly built from galvanised iron which takes on many shapes to form shelter under adverse conditons. The high ceilings in these shops serves for additional ventilation and the use of lattice on the verandah favours additional shade. There is no glass in windows, only shutters which are propped to catch the breeze.

Broome is a long way from most places. Its very geographical condition conjures exotic thoughts of deserts, stretches of white sand and beach, pearling luggers and loneliness.

Broome was founded in 1864 when Alex Forrest, the late Lord Forrest's brother, visited the Kimberlies and, on his return trip, Roebuck Bay. Forrest saw the possibilities of the harbour and realised its potential as a port for the entire north-west—certainly no better harbour had been discovered at that stage. In accordance with the best traditions and legends of the time, Forrest declared Broome a townsite. The Kimberlies were a revelation to Forrest and he quickly realised the potential of these lands for pastoral settlement and, in the future, agriculture. The townsite was declared formally in 1883 and named in honour of Sir Fredrick Napier Broome, Governor of Western Australia between 1883 and 1889.

Mother-of-pearl shell had already been noticed lying around the shores of Roebuck Bay and this stimulated the interest of the early settlers and finally established a pearl shell industry. In Broome the tide rises some thirty feet and at low tide the water line recedes, in some places, up to a mile. Gathering pearl shell was therefore a simple matter. After a time, this operation became restricted in the immediate area of Broome and gathering in the deep waters of the bay was impossible without sophisticated diving equipment.

The main pearl grounds in the early days were on Ninety-Mile Beach, a long stretch of coastline with a sandy bottom, and from here a great harvest of pearl and mother-of-pearl was collected. In the early days the supply seemed inexhaustible. At first the local native divers were used to harvest the pearl shell, but by the early 1900s conventional diving dress had been introduced and this brought an influx of Asiatics who proved adept in the use of the equipment. Manilamen, Japanese, Malays, Chinese and Koepangers came and took the place of the local men. Broome at that time became the established centre of the pearling industry in Australia and fleets of luggers scoured the north-west coast of Western Australia in search of pearl shells and pearls.

At the height of the pearling days, just prior to the Second World War, 400 luggers operated from Broome, employing 3,000 men of a population exceeding 5,000 persons.

Broome was laid out on a gridiron pattern which tends to become monotonous as there are very few civic amenities, open spaces or town planning disciplines. The town relies on a more exotic flavour of architecture for its interest, particularly the adaption of diverse architectural types to this harsh environment. The housing is like any housing in Australia except for the

Above & right
Along the coastal waters of Broome there are massive tides. In the early days, coastal boats were designed with flat bottoms so that they could gently come to rest on the ocean floor. Today a deep water wharf has been constructed.

extremely wide verandahs which cast deep shadows. 'On the verandah' said one observer at the turn of the century, writing his memoirs in an article called 'Compensations' 'let it be said that no one who knows Southern Australia only, knows what a real verandah is—nor a real hammock.' The phrase 'sunny verandah' is a contradiction in term. A verandah is for shade and coolness—nothing narrower than eight feet is worth its name.

The houses in Broome are vernacular and bear the imprints of pioneering. They are simply furnished, if not spartan, for good furniture would be wasted. In the dry season the dust drifts thickly in and abrades the surface. Wood, which was a few weeks earlier swollen with damp, will crack with heat, looking glasses will mildew after a year and curtains are superfluous as they take up too much of the breeze. The architecture therefore is relaxed, tropical, and open in plan. Windows invariably go to the floor and are always open, except during storms. The verandah, furnished with pot plants and cane and canvas chairs, is used most of the time.

Houses are mostly timber structures with a corrugated iron sheeted roof. The verandah may have lattice or louvres, or a variety of ventilating systems. In a few of the older houses, the floors are of polished jarrah—the native mahogany-coloured timber—upon which light mats only are placed.

Broome in 1942, and to a less certain extent today, had a colourful market. Lyndall Stuart-Hadow in an article in *Walkabout* (1 January 1942) said: '. . . small, dark-skinned, black-haired women in tiny-waisted blouses and voluminous skirts, bustle among the oily boarding house-masters and their bargains obtained, clatter away in their wooden sandals to disappear into one of the numerous swarming lanes of "the Quarter".' The 'Quarter' can be compared with colourful Dixon Street in Sydney where merchants and cafes, grocers and Chinese cake shops jostle with each other for business. In Broome the distance from the Orient can easily be forgotten.

The Second World War brought about an almost complete cessation of pearling activities due to the absence of the Japanese divers. After the Second World War the industry revived and production steadily increased until 1957 when forty-seven luggers harvested 991 tons of shell valued at £1,209,602 and pearls worth £19,786. By 1963, only six luggers were operational but this has slightly increased due to the demand for live pearl shell for the cultured pearl industry.

204

In 1956, 250 miles north of Broome, a cultured pearl industry was established and now the luggers collect the young live shells and ship them to the various pearl farms. New cultured pearl farms have also been established south of Broome.

With the advent of closer settlement in the Kimberley district, Broome has become an important meat processing centre. The town will probably continue to grow as a new steel and concrete port was built in 1966 and ships of 20,000 tons can take meat direct from Broome to the United States, Japan, Singapore and other countries. This obviated the old system when flat bottom vessels had to be used because of the dramatic change in tide. In old photographs it is not unusual to see a large vessel standing dry.

Broome is Australia's piece of Asia and with a bit of imagination it is not difficult to believe you are other than in Australia, especially when you see a tri-shaw, the lonely little Japanese cemetery or the abundance of Chinese cafés and stores which are operating in this tropical port.

In the roaring days of Broome when the pearl industry was staffed mainly by Japanese and Malay divers, an active 'foreign quarter' existed with Joss houses, restaurants and boarding houses. Today remnants of this quarter exist but much of the vitality has gone with the decline of the pearling industry. On the outskirts of Broome are the Japanese graves.

Right
The architecture in Broome varies with use but generally the severity of the climate dictates its form. All buildings have verandahs to shelter the walls frum the tremendous heat. There is little glass in buildings but mainly renewable wall sections capable of being raised or lowered according to the degree of ventilation.

Over left
The evidence of the multi-racial population can be seen in many buildings which sometimes combine with the Australian vernacular in curious forms such as in the Japanese Club.

Over right
The Court House at Broome is a restrained vernacular building constructed from corrugated iron with a cast iron verandah including columns and steps. The ventilation ridge is a device used in the tropics to expel hot air from the roof area.

Charters Towers

Queensland

A view of Charters Towers from the Day Dawn Claim (when the mines were still in operation), an etching by J. R. Ashton.

Right
Charters Towers main street. The broad walk has been preserved complete with verandahs supported by delicate cast iron columns and infill panels of iron lace.

One can get to Charters Towers, the notorious mining town, by three trains in the day . . . The country one passes through is not striking. It is just bushland with grass, cactus, aloe, fern and eucalyptus. Some good bits of pastoral country appear here and there, and there is a small settlement at many places on the line, but it does not seem a district of great possibilities. A fine range of hills is climbed, but they are just what one crosses in a score of places in New South Wales or Victoria . . . The 82 miles travelled could be slept over without much loss, unless one was counting, with a prospector's eye, on the possibilities of minerals in the hills and the sudden outcrops.

So wrote a miner in his memoirs in 1889.

Gold was discovered here in 1872 by a party of miners who included Messrs Mosman, Clarke and Fraser. They were attracted by a number of small peaks in the distance which took on the form of medieval castle towers, and they determined to explore them. They rode through seventeen miles of well-grassed and lightly-timbered country until they reached the largest of the hills which was about 300 feet high. Around its base they found considerable quantities of quartz richly impregnated with gold. Each of them marked out a claim and reported the discovery to the nearest gold warden, Mr Charters, who visited the locality. He was satisfied that the find was genuine and valuable and granted the prospectors such reward claims as were allowed at that time.

The goldfield, an area of granite and syenite bordered by areas of slate and grits, occupies the western edge of the Charters Towers district. Around the town the soil is sandy and porous and, except around the creeks, little suited to cultivation. This lack of good agricultural land was compensated for by land westward, running for hundreds of miles, which still supports immense herds of cattle and flocks of sheep.

The town was typical of many of the gold rush towns with its pubs and banks, mostly constructed from timber, flanking the main street. The town in 1890 boasted four banks: the Bank of New South Wales, Australian Joint Stock Bank, Queensland National Bank and the Bank of Australasia. There were eight churches: two Anglican, two Roman Catholic, one Methodist, one Presbyterian, one Wesleyan and one Lutheran. The town was serviced with three State schools—boys, girls and mixed—and had as well the local parish school for the Roman Catholic population.

To complete the inventory of the town, Charters Towers had (like every other town) the inevitable School of Arts with a circulating library of 2,500 volumes. It is still a proud building

The Australian Bank of Commerce is designed in the Renaissance style with Greek orders, but here architecture has been adapted to the tropics especially in the use of open colonnades.

Right
The Australian Bank of Commerce can be seen in the distance. In the middle section is a great barrel vault of iron forming an imposing entrance to a shop. Next to this is the City Hall designed in the Renaissance manner.

Most Victorian towns were not complete without a park and bandstand. At weekends amusements were simple and the band used to perform regularly playing excerpts from Gilbert and Sullivan and military airs and marches.

Right
A dignified and simple townscape is created by verandahs and its aesthetic appeal cannot be underestimated. The verandah forms a transitional element between nature and built form, softening the architecture and creating a more organic unit.

within the town and in former days boasted of a good sized reading room 'which was supplied with the principal papers and periodicals of the day.'

There were meeting halls built in the town centre for the Protestant sects of Masons and Oddfellows, as well as other lodges, and a jockey club which held two race meetings a year.

Gold mining was the main activity in Charters Towers but there were other industries during those roaring days. There was an iron foundry and engineering works, a soap works and a brewery situated on the Burdekin River. Timber for construction was brought in by rail and bullock teams from twenty miles away. Agriculture was exclusively carried out by the Chinese community. By the turn of the century the Chinese population was about 500.

Charters Towers was therefore quite sufficient, unlike most of the gold rush towns, especially in the west, which had to rely on goods and provisions, and sometimes even water, being hauled in from distant areas.

The main street of Charters Towers is slightly bent, but for the most part the town follows a gridiron pattern of subdivision. The street is reasonably wide and has a comfortable scale created by two-storey buildings. The centre of the town can be assumed to be around the Post Office where the strong Italianate tower with clock dominates. This building is typical of the post offices built at that time, Italianate detailing in painted stucco. They are robust buildings and perhaps the best pieces of Victorian civic architecture.

Across the road from the Post Office is a strange Art Nouveau building of Stan Pollard & Co. It is a symmetrical building with two flanking open octagonals acting as pylons to an immense arch. The hoarding to the street has its own zig-zag rhythm with counterpoint created by the descriptions of hosiery, drapery, etc., in bold colour. These buildings have enormous value as they are the vernacular interpretation of high style architecture. The more subtle issues of Mackintosh have been lost but an architecture of vigour has replaced it. Most of the banks and other commercial buildings have been designed in the Renaissance manner but with a more three-dimensional effect by creating verandahs and patios of considerable depth. The Australian Bank of Commerce is an example of this as is the City Hall which is Palladian in detail. The building is restrained and designed with a central arched portal, with surmounting pediment. The first floor is also arcaded with the central bay emphasised by coupled columns. To complete the Palladian style the parapets have balustrades in the appropriate manner.

OUNTER - LUNCH
12pm - 1·30pm
MBURGERS - 25c
CKET OF CHIPS - 2
ried Chicken, Chips
+ Salad 7
rry + Rice 7
R. DUCKWORTH.
GOLDEN CASKET AGENT.
TAILOR.
CALEDONIAN HOUSE
PEDESTRIAN
CROSSING
AHEAD
DRY
CLEANERS
NZA·93

Mosman Street, Charters Towers, in 1874, from a painting by Mr Adam in the possession of Mr J. Oxman. The variety of diggers can be seen—Chinese, Military people, labourers, city clerks— all with one intention, to make money and to find their luck.

Timber is used widely in Queensland and its use in this Roman Catholic Church has an almost joyous expression. The complex structure of the bell tower contrasts well with the simple neo-Gothic church.

Right
The store of Stan Pollard and Co. is a strange expression of Art Nouveau architecture and plays a most important role in the streetscape. The towers are rather Gothic and much needed visually to restrain the movement created by so large an arch. The slight zigzag treatment to the verandah, with corresponding sign writing, is whimsical and reflects the amateur interpretation of the style.

Charters Towers feels as if the gold rush is still on. The buildings have that sense of urgency and glittering mantle. 'Fitzgerald's Hotel' has mirrored swing doors to the bars and sports more mirrored advertisements on its outside walls. The upstairs verandah is deep and shaded with a simple criss-cross balcony rail detail. In other parts of the main street, the shop fronts are protected by large verandahs supported on elegant, slim, cast iron columns with a variety of versions of Greek order capitals. Spandrel panels are filled with a riot of cast iron details of flower patterns and a Greek flavour is often expressed with inverted Anthemion and Acroterion motives which hang like a lace curtain from their structural supports. Along the pavement areas, the columns of some of the shops display traditional advertising—the barber naturally has striped his columns with red and white diagonals symbolising the blood and bandage of former times.

The houses within the town are typical of Queensland. Most of them are built from timber and many of them raised off the ground. There have been many theories advanced as to why the Queensland house was raised one storey. Some say they were elevated from the soil on timber piles to get away from the marauding white ant which could eat its way through timber foundations if undetected; others say the living areas were placed in the air to get away from the heat of the soil and in the hope of catching a breeze. There is a fascination in the architecture of these houses; a feeling of the tropics which other translations of European architecture have not achieved; the simple treatment of the verandah with adjustable louvres to catch the slightest zephyr, and the large space on the ground floor used for a variety of purposes.

Lattice was also used by the less affluent and usually surrounded the whole house. In the more primitive examples the entire house could consist of a series of flaps constructed from timber or galvanised iron which could adjust to ventilation requirements. When fully opened they created a sense of some great lizard with its breathing gills open for air.

There are a few miners left in the town. Their galvanised iron sheds are reminders of the former activity. The truth, simplicity and dignity of these structures are beginning to be appreciated more. Form follows function, structure is used sparingly, roofs poise daintily on their members ready to dance across the landscape.

The mines have all virtually closed but fortunately the town has not died—it is now the centre of a considerable pastoral, dairying and citrus growing district.

Once the 'Park Hotel' and now a residence, this architecture has been expressly designed for the tropics. It has copious verandahs with shutters and adjustable louvres to keep off the sun and regulate the breezes. The roof has an absence of chimneys but in their place, galvanised ventilators whirl.

Functional necessity and rude simplicity is expressed in this house. Some of the features of Queensland architecture are illustrated here, such as the elevated living area, the flexible wall system created by metal blades capable of catching breezes and the hipped roof, typical of many Queensland homes.

Right
The roaring days are all here. Glass mirrored swing doors and wide verandahs were typical of so many of these hotels. The 'Excelsior Hotel' is one of the many hotels surviving from the gold rush days.

Ravenswood

Queensland

In the *Illustrated Sydney News and Supplement* the following article appeared.

Ravenswood is a mining township in North Queensland. It contains a money-order office, savings bank and telegraph office. . . It is almost entirely a quartz-reefing district, and bids fair to become a place of great importance. In 1871 the yield of gold was 62,000 ounces, of which only about one tenth was from the alluvial diggings. Copper and galena are also found in large quantities. The number of miners' rights issued during the year was 2,334. The Bank of New South Wales has established an agency at Ravenswood, and the Joint Stock Bank also possesses a branch. The "Ravenswood Miner" is the local journal. The population, including the Chinese, is estimated to be about 2,000. The churches comprise an Anglican and a Roman Catholic edifice. Hotels are well represented, being thirteen in number. The public buildings comprise a court house, a national school, and a school of arts. The climate . . . is very healthy. . . Ravenswood is reached by coach, which runs twice a week from Townsville, the nearest sea port, distant 75 miles.

Gold was discovered on the Ravenswood River by Messrs Curr, Carr and Cunningham. On the Curr Brothers' cattle station, 'Merree Merreewar', a hand called Thomas Aitken induced a party of three on a prospecting expedition along the Ravenswood River. After leaving Townsville and travelling towards the Burdekin River they met Mr Marmaduke Carr who told them of likely country for prospecting where he had picked up some gold-bearing quartz. They took Mr Carr's advice and commenced prospecting on Connolly Creek.

One of that party describes the eventful day:

We were soon on the spot, the grass being much better there, and plenty of water, and formed our camp on the same side of Connolly Creek, only a few hundred yards lower down. This was about the middle of October, 1868. One day, at the end of the month, Brooks appeared at our tent door, his face all smiles, and carrying a miner's prospecting dish, his eyes fixed on the bottom, and judging from the expression on his face, it might have been full of minted sovereigns. He had come to let us know, and to show us, about a half ounce of gold which he had got in one dish full of wash-dirt taken from a gully not very far away.

This find was called Tucker Gully and at the head of this gully the Perseverance, Donnybrook and other reefs were discovered. The Perseverance was the first gold claim to be granted.

Curr had procured a few ounces of gold from the prospectors in payment for rations. He was a business man and anxious to find a ready market for his produce and what better way to do this than have a gold rush and a thriving town near one's property. Curr went into Bowen with the ore and advertised it well. On his return he was followed by half the town.

Detail of the verandah of one of the two remaining hotels in Ravenswood. The turned columns and the louvred swing doors with inset mirrors give some indication of the former glory of these structures.

Right
The roaring days have gone, the streets are now quiet, but the spirit of the gold rush lingers on in hotels which were almost palaces in these bustling mining days. The hotel was the most opulent and important building in town and this can be easily appreciated at Ravenswood. This was the 'Imperial Hotel.'

A further find was made on the watershed of Elphinstone Creek, the spot where Ravenswood now stands. The early photographs show Ravenswood in the 1870s with rude timber buildings. The floors of the early dwellings were usually a clay pug modelled and then trampled into a suitably hard state, but some simple dwellings contained a rude timber floor. The walls were constructed from split logs lodged in a rough frame. The roof was constructed from round saplings covered with bark sheets tied down with bullock hide and further secured by additional poles strapped to both ridge and eaves board. Some buildings had corrugated iron, but for the most part bark slabs dominated the scene.

The progression of architecture appears to have been canvas, then timber and if the diggings were profitable a permanent town of bricks and mortar was built. For the most part however, in the regions out of town, calico was the common material for housing.

The diggers' residence was commonly a small calico tent on the slopes of the gully where the claim was, and the area occupied by it was twelve by eight. There were many canvas tents and a few log huts, and some had rude chimneys. The furniture consisted of one or two stumps of trees for chairs, while anything in the shape of a box or tea chest served as a table. The bed consisted of a stretcher or bunk made of forked stakes and saplings covered with a rug and a pair or two of blankets. The cooking utensils were few, and intended to wear well. There were two or three tin or pewter plates, spoons, knives and forks (although the latter were not always present). Two or three saucepans and one or two billies, generally completed the list, while a frying-pan was regarded as a luxury.

In *Missing Friends* by T. P. Weitemeyer, who travelled the goldfields between 1871–80 and who subtitled his book *Being the Adventures of a Danish Immigrant in Queensland* says:

. . . I saw the township of Ravenswood lying before me. I stopped the horses to have a look . . . At last I was on a gold field. What a magic spell there seemed to be in the words . . . There was an ordinary street composed of hotels, boarding houses and stores, on both sides of the road. Behind the street were tents in which the diggers principally lived. Everywhere were earth mounds where some one had been busy rooting the ground about. The reefs were each surmounted by an ordinary windlass where a man would stand hauling up the quartz all day long. Such was the picture at a superficial glance at Ravenswood and I think the description answers for all other Queensland gold-diggings.

Weitemeyer talks about the numerous hotels (but these seemed to be more drinking houses as the Chinese boarding houses had the residential trade), and the way the shopkeepers of the town would take a waggon load of goods and take them to the diggings for quick profit.

Ravenswood in 1873.

But now it is a ghost town the dust lies heavy in its streets. Most of the pubs are shut and deserted, the shops are completely empty and doors and windows flap in the breeze. Only a few inhabitants keep the old town just ticking along. And yet what an experience it is to walk down this street today to see the magnificent hotels, once filled with pride and joyous expression of architectural detail and nonsense, standing like grand palaces.

The 'Imperial Hotel' in Ravenswood is one of the finest and was built to last for many centuries, and for that matter will most probably do so. The architecture is a piece of Victorian virtuoso—large arches are a parcel of the vocabulary used on the ground floor with infill lattice spandrels and turned columns of sugar candy design. The first floor is more flamboyant with primitive corinthian capitals constructed from timber. The parapets of the hotel are extremely high and broken up by stupa forms. In the centre of the composition stands a raised portion with segmental arch on which the name of the hotel proudly stands. As if this was not enough!—the masonry was also designed in 'blood and bandage' (the architectural expression given to the alternate layers of red and cream brickwork). The doors are mirrored with cotton reel decoration on the top.

Inside the 'Imperial Hotel' it is dark and comfortable, woodwork glows with an aged patina and, on the bar, china pulls were used to drag the draught beer from the cellar.

The 'Railway Hotel' is similarly opulent but has less flamboyance in its architectural details, nevertheless it expresses the same features of two-storey verandah façade surrounding a brick shell, and parapets concealing the entire roof pattern.

The Ravenswood Post Office is a simple classical affair which once had open verandahs which are now filled in by boards to effect more accommodation. The entrance sports a portico with pediment. The Ambulance Station is more robust with a large segmental arch over the garage and has a simple fenestration pattern. There are simple timber churches inspired by the 'Carpenter's Gothic', and remains of shops and sundry commercial buildings all of which can give a picture of the glorious past.

Around the town are mullock heaps from the mines, vast heaps of dirt and stone, remains of derricks, bits of shed and remnants of cottages. The scene is ghostly and romantic. In the hot sunlight, the colours in the architecture have faded, timber has weathered to a silver grey, the brickwork has a film of dust remaining from the last storm, the streets are stoned and rutted. Nothing happens now and only the dreams of the old goldfields linger.

224

Derricks and chimneys—parts of the
past—lay scattered amidst the ruins of
old buildings. Ravenswood today is
a ghost town.

Right
The sculptured qualities of the early
buildings should be appreciated.
Parapets concealed the roofs of commercial
buildings in a variety of ways, and
verandahs could be either cantilevered or
supported on columns depending
upon the width of cover. The
building in the centre is the School of Arts
and the local theatre is to the far left.

Childers

Queensland

The main street of Childers. Established trees, now one of the main features of the town, were small and guarded by rails when this photograph was taken. On the right hand side of the street there is a dominance of commercial architecture whilst on the left a more residential quality exists.

Right
A nervous skyline is very much a part of the urbanscape of Childers. Pediments, scrolls, vases, urns, top knots, acroterion, and even curving supporting scrolls, reminiscent of Dutch Baroque Architecture, can be seen.

Originally it was known as Isis Scrub and inhabited by pastoralists and squatters on runs of up to thirty or forty square miles in area.

Gold was discovered on Stanton Harcourt's run in the eighties and although not immediately a rich find it gave sufficient stimulus to the area to make it popular and bring in settlers.

William Howard was the first white man to explore the Isis Scrub—thickly-timbered land on rich, red, volcanic soil. Howard arrived from England in 1857 and visited the area with the expressed desire to explore the Scrub.

The hoop pine trees in this area attracted a large number of settlers and allied industries such as charcoal burners who transported the charcoal to the Bundaberg mills and the Maryborough gas works at Aldershot. When the land was cleared of the timber, crops such as corn and pumpkins were planted.

The chief town in the Isis Scrub, situated in the heart of the old scrub area, is Childers. The town of Childers was named after the Right Honourable H. Childers, Agent-General for Victoria between 1857 and 1860.

In most settlements in Australia, transportation plays an important part. Towns are established at the junctions of transportation systems, be they roads or river, and Childers' birth was very much dependent on the railway construction north. As settlement increased in the scrub area a railway was completed to transport the hoop pine timber to market. The railway between Howard and Goodwood was completed in 1887 and passed through a siding known as Isis Junction. The line from Isis Junction to Childers was completed in 1887 (subsequently closed in 1964) and from Goodwood to Bundaberg in 1888.

The first buildings at Childers were an hotel, a blacksmith's shop and a butcher's shop. In the *Sum of our Yesterdays*, Iris Thompson says:

. . . the railway station became a meeting place and a getting together of the district residents to collect railway freight and the mail. Perhaps the most pressing reason for the get together was to enable the settlers to enjoy the company of their fellows, to discuss the crops, the weather, and the other important topics of the day. Perhaps those early meetings at the railway were the forerunner of today's club or brotherhood movement.

With the expansion of the railway into the scrub area, and the construction of the railway to Childers itself, the town quickly grew. In 1891 the population was ninety-one and by the turn of the century had grown to 4,000 persons. The shire of Isis was proclaimed in 1903 with an

Verandahs adorned with lattice throw complex shadows but reduce a building's three-dimensional quality. The dual stair leading to the verandah is a typical North Queensland detail.

Right
Within a town there is generally an architectural oddity—Childers is no exception. This strange residence has proportions almost Cyclopian and yet the scale of the building appears to be diminutive, probably caused by the bold detailing. It could be called an example of carpenter's Renaissance and appropriately was a masonic club.

area of 677 square miles and the town centre shifted from the town of Howard to Childers.

The shire's economy had been based entirely upon cattle, timber getting and a few cereal crops such as corn and pumpkin growing, until experiments were carried out by J. E. Noakes to grow sugar cane in the district. It had previously been thought that sugar growing was unsuitable as the area was too dry. However, Noakes' experiment paid off, his crops successful, and sugar reached the sum of £38 a ton. This set the pattern for others to follow and allied industries and sugar mills were established.

By the 1890s most of the land was being put into cane production and as the scrub was cleared the riches of the soil unfolded. Kanaka labour was used extensively in the fields. This cheap labour was introduced into Queensland in 1863 and persisted until 1901.

In 1893 the Isis cane growers were told by the Colonial Sugar Refining Company of their intention to build a mill in the area. The mill commenced operations in 1895 and was rivalled only by the Isis Central Mill which was inaugurated in 1893. This mill offered the opportunity to farmers to co-operate in a system whereby they shared in the profits. The Isis Central Mill was erected in 1897 and thirty properties supplied the cane. When the mills first operated the cane was hauled in by waggon and dray, but later narrow gauge tram lines were laid to pick-up points where cane was brought by waggon and thence to the mill.

The early trams were drawn by horses but these were superseded by locomotives in 1900.

Today the trains still run burdened with heavy loads of sugar cane. The tracks meander around the town and across the fields and in season they represent a busy sight. Childers itself is quiet in contrast to the activity which appears on the canefields and represents, for the most part, a rural centre which has grown steadily over the years, although the bulk of its buildings are of the Victorian era.

The main street, being slightly curved, gives rise to many and varied forms of architectural composition. The shopping centre is slightly Baroque with its roof expressions hidden behind decorative parapets consisting of pediments, consoles, false fronts—in fact every conceivable architectural device which can be mustered to give effect. Yet these forms are exciting and certainly stimulate the townscape by giving it a high Victorian character. Verandahs for the most part shade the footpath, but in some instances these have been replaced by cantilevered awnings. Where older verandahs exist, additional shade has been achieved by drop canvas awning blinds which give a gay atmosphere to the street.

The National Bank of Childers is a typical interpretation of classical architecture translated into the timber vernacular. The pediment and parapet indicate a primitive frontier architecture.

Right
The main street of Childers. The slight bend in the street suggests mystery and intrigue which a straight street can never offer. There is an element of expectation in the curve, a change of architectural composition which invariably delights in new arrangement.

In the centre of the street are trees of a mature nature which break the monotony of the ribbon development of the shopping centre and at the same time create civic spaces for shade and sometimes shelter motor cars from the sun.

What gives Childers a quality which many Queensland towns lack? It may be the quantity of tropical trees abounding in the streets and gardens or the quality of the Victorian architecture which to some degree expresses a tropical feeling especially with the play of light and shadow of lattice and verandah. Perhaps also there is a blandness and a naive quality in the architecture found nowhere else in Australia.

Throughout the town there are simple vernacular buildings such as the Court House, built from timber, supporting a combination of pitched and hipped roofs and simple verandahs with lattice screens. The building is unpretentious and modest, sheltering behind large trees and lawns.

The Post Office expresses the same feeling and is similarly constructed from weatherboard. Each window has a hood projecting from the wall with the sides filled in with lattice. The National Bank in Childers follows the theme further in a classical interpretation. The building is symmetrical about the central doorway and balanced by windows, all of which are sheltered by a broad verandah. The roof of this structure is totally concealed by a timber parapet and truncated pediment of a type, which is terminated by pilasters.

There are many other timber buildings with verandahs where the façade is restricted by a vocabulary of timber and this gives a particular expression. The sub-branch R.S.S.A.I.L.A. Club, for example, has segmental arches formed in timber with spandrels filled in with lattice decoration. The ground floor of this building has a valance board composed of quite intricate timber fretwork which is repeated between the ground floor and the natural ground level.

In and about the town are certain architectural follies, structures amusing because of their pomposity or their striving to attain high style architecture. Usually they fail visually and through siting and circumstance can only be treated as architectural jokes. Other buildings within the town attain a level of serious architectural interpretation.

Most of the architecture and town planning in Childers is simple, honest and consistent and, as a town which grew out of a need for settlement, it represents one of the best.

Some buildings in Childers have an elegance and a delicacy rare in timber buildings. There is a feeling of tropical architecture in the wide verandahs which is seen in small details such as ventilators between the ground and verandah deck.

Right
Main street of Childers.

Normanton

Queensland

Normanton did not quite reach expectations for the honour of being the capital of the north of Queensland. Today it remains a country town which cattle trucks use as a stopover.

Right
The urbanscape of Normanton is typical of outback towns where the skyline consists of windmills and tank stands which take on proportions greater than reality when seen in this flat landscape.

It could hardly be said that Normanton is on the tourist route; however, the town is accessible by road and by air and is worth the effort just to experience its remoteness. There is a sense of drama, a sense of loneliness that typifies so many of the towns in 'the back of beyond'. Normanton is situated about fifty miles from the mouth of the Norman River and is built on low ironstone ridges which are common in northern Queensland. The Australian United Steam Navigation Company Limited *Handbook* says:
Vital statistics prove the town to be healthy, which is at variance with the general opinion in the South. The population is about 600; a few years ago it was about 1,400, but the attractions of the Croydon and Georgetown goldfields have considerably reduced it.

The factors needed to improve transportation links with the outside world are clearly enunciated in the *Handbook*. The decline of Normanton as an important town can be clearly appreciated considering the lack of communications and the lure of mining to the south. The decline was aggravated further by the finds of rich deposits of ore at Mt Isa in recent years. Mt Isa has continually eclipsed Normanton as a centre of importance in north-western Queensland.

The town was originally opened by settlers as a port for the cattle stations on the Flinders and Cloncurry Rivers. It was to replace Burketown which is located some 100 miles to the west on the Albert River. Burketown also suffered from its isolation and its difficulty of access.

The Norman River was named by Landsborough after the captain of the Victorian Government ship, *Victoria*. The river is reasonably deep and Messrs Landsborough and G. Phillips were the first to navigate it in January 1867. They chose the site for the township of Normanton on the left side of the river where some high ironstone ridges come close to the river. This site was chosen as it was easy to drain, free from flooding and was immediately accessible to the back country of the Flinders River system.

Among the first to settle in the town was Dr Borck, a popular medical practitioner. An hotel was among the first buildings and was built by Mr A. McLennan who had been concerned with the early settlement of Burketown. Mr Ellis Read, trading for R. Towns and Co., soon had a store established and carried on a brisk business with the stations and the miners on the Etheridge River—and so a town was started.

Normanton soon became the port for shipping wool to Sydney. The first wool team to

The 'National Hotel' is an opulent structure surrounded by verandahs. The hotel, especially for country people travelling long distances from outback stations, forms the nucleus for social intercourse.

Right
The 'Central Hotel' is a simple vernacular building not unlike early New South Wales or Tasmanian buildings where the limitation of materials dictated their form. This is especially evident in the roof which consists of two hip roofs rather than a single span to avoid long lengths of timber.

Over left & right
The quiet brooding which isolation and heat generate, and the protection of the verandah, can easily be appreciated in the far north of Australia, especially in Normanton.

arrive in town was driven from Saxby at the head of the Norman River and from then on wool arrived from 'Donor's Hills' and other stations on the Flinders. Even as early as 1868 wool was shipped to Sydney by any chance vessel that happened to berth.

Normanton is included in this book for its spatial qualities. Buildings are placed with large areas of land around them and are seen in isolation rather than in groups. Only in this country where deserts abound is the skyline so important. Windmills and water tanks form giant sculptural shapes against the sky and this condition is reinforced all the time by the incredible flatness and desolation of the surrounding terrain.

There are no buildings of historic quality, there are no buildings of real architectural merit, but there are buildings which express humour such as M. Loy's general store with a hanging sign which jauntily crosses his verandah and conceals a multitude of building sins. The Burns, Philp & Co. Store stands on one corner of the town with three repeating arches displaying the name of the company with the shop and store sheltered by a slender timber and iron verandah. There is a touch of Walt Disney about this architecture, an over-simplification of what may have been an original boastful attempt of the serious.

Visually the most prominent building in town is the hotel on the corner of the main street. A lofty edifice encircled by timber verandahs and fitted with iron lace work, the strangely-proportioned pub sits proudly on the ground giving the impression that it is about to take off. The 'Central Hotel' is a much more modest structure with two hipped roof structures joined together by a verandah. It is reminiscent of very early Georgian roof construction, the details of which were necessitated by the scarcity of long lengths of structural timber which caused the break-up of the roof into smaller components. The other hotel in town is a large structure built over many stages but unified by consistent balustrade and verandah details.

Today the cattle trucks roll in from the far-reaching properties, their drivers thirsty after the long desolate drive across the desert, and so the town does a reasonable trade with hotels—there is little else except drink in the hotels to quench the intolerable thirst which the far north engenders. The drivers yarn with the locals on how Normanton may have been the capital of the north.

238

Bibliography

ROSS

Kermode, R. L., Ross Centenary, June 2nd 1821 to June 2nd 1921.
Von Strieglitz, K. R., A Short History of Ross.

OATLANDS

Von Strieglitz, K. R., A History of Oatlands and Jericho, *1960.*

EVANDALE

Von Strieglitz, K. R., Days and Ways in Old Evandale.
Von Strieglitz, K. R., History of Evandale, *Birchalls 1967.*

RICHMOND

Von Strieglitz, K. R., Richmond, the story of its people and its places, *Launceston Telegraph Printery, 1953.*
Rowlands, W., Richmond's 100 Years of Municipal Government, *published by the author, 1961.*
Skemp, J. R., Letters to Anne, *Melbourne University Press, 1956.*
West, History of Tasmania.
Jones, E., Excursion to Richmond, Saturday 17th September, 1966, *Tasmanian Historical Research Association Inc.*

BERRIMA

Jervis, J., Berrima, *Royal Australian Historical Society, Journal and Proceedings, Vol. 13, 1947.*
Jervis, J., A History of the Berrima District 1798–1961, *issued by the Berrima County Council, Berrima 1962.*
Roxburgh, R., A Brief History of Berrima, New South Wales, *produced by the Berrima Village Trust, Edwards and Shaw, 1969.*
Small, W. Y., Reminiscences of Gaol Life at Berrima, *1923.*

CARCOAR

Lenehan, M., Carcoar, Mother Town of the Lachlan Valley.
Steel, W. A., The Churches of Carcoar, *Royal Australian Historical Society Journal and Proceedings, Vol. 17, 1931.*
Steel, W. A., History of Carcoar, 1815–1881, *Royal Australian Historical Society Journal and Proceedings, Vol. 17, 1931.*

GULGONG

Bourke, E., Gold and Silver, *Kodak 1953–54.*

Jones, L. J., & Rayner, Y. N., The Gulgong Gold Fields, *New South Wales Survey of Mineral Resources, No. 38.*

Maxwell, Eileen, Written in Gold, *Mudgee Guardian, 1959.*

Pike, A., Gulgong Diamond Deposits, *Austral-Brita, 1917.*

Claridge, W. M., A History of Gulgong, *notes published Gulgong, 1940.*

SILVERTON

Bridges, R., From Silver to Steel, The Romance of the Broken Hill Proprietary Company, *1920.*

Curtis, L. S., History of Broken Hill, *1908.*

Farwell, George, Ghost Towns of Australia, *Nelson, 1965.*

Meggy, P. R., Sydney to Silverton, *1885.*

Barrier Miners Business Directory, 1891–2.

Oakes, Rev. Y. S., Round and About, *bush sketches, Mitchell Library Collection.*

BRAIDWOOD

Back to Braidwood, *Official Souvenir, November 19–26, 1966.*

WILCANNIA

Daniels, Rev. L., Far West, *Sydney Church of England Information Trust, 1959.*

Oakes, Rev. Y. S., Round and About, *bush sketches, Mitchell Library Collection.*

Proud, C., Murray and Darling Trade in *1882.*

Back to Wilcannia, *souvenir book, Sydney, John Sands, 1939.*

BENDIGO

Bendigo City Council, 1855–1905. A resume of Municipal Progress, *issued by A. Dunstan, Mayor, Lyttleton Terrace, Victoria. J. B. Young, publisher, 1905.*

Bracken, T., Dear old Bendigo, Victoria, *Robshaw, 1892.*

Yormly, J., Reminiscences, *Vol. 3.*

Kimberly, W. G., Bendigo & Vicinity, *1895.*

Mackay, G., Annals of Bendigo, 1851 to 1891. *Melbourne, Mackay & Co., 1891.*

Vahland, W. G., History of Freemasonry in the Bendigo District, *1909.*

Walker, T., 'Early days in Bendigo'. New Nation Magazine, *June, 1931.*

MALDON

Advance Maldon Association. Picturesque Maldon (the Centenary record of Victoria's celebrated
gold fields and fertile district), *Published Wilson & Zenne, Times Office.*

Bradford, W., Maldon Gold Field, *1904.*

Williams, A. J., Concise History of Maldon and the Tarrangower diggings, Maldon. *R. T.
Wilson, 1953.*

Dunn, E. J., Some Gold Mines at Maldon, Victorian *Geological Survey Records, Vol. 2.*

BEECHWORTH

Beechworth Progress Association, Illustrated guide to Beechworth and Vicinity.

Harvey, Ray, 'Background to Beechworth 1852–1952'. Beechworth, Ovens and Murray
Advertiser, *1952.*

National Trust of Australia (Vic.), Visit Historic Beechworth, *Melbourne, 1966.*

Warren & Co., Beechworth Directory, *1857.*

PORT FAIRY

Tyers, G., Early days in South Western Victoria, *Victorian Historical Magazine, Vol. 12, 1928.*

Belfast, *Directory of Victoria, 1851.*

Earle, W., Port Fairy Victoria, *Published Port Fairy Gazette Office, 1896.*

Mills, O., Why Should their Honour Fade, *Hawthorn Press, 1960.*

Port Fairy Gazette, *Centenary Issue, 1949.*

BURRA

Perry, M., & Auhl, I, Burra Sketchbook, *Rigby Limited, 1970*

Burgess, Rev. H. J., Cyclopedia of South Australia, *Vol. 2, 1909.*

Alvey, Rev. H., Burra, Its Mines and Methodism. *Back to Burra celebrations, October 1936.*

Treloar, Frank, Burra Mine: Reminiscences of its Rise and Fall, *1845–1871.*

MINTARO

The information for Mintaro is contained generally in The History of Burra.

STRATHALBYN

Adams, W., and Jones, L., Back to Strathalbyn, *1933.*

Henn, L., & Co., Views of South Australia.

GOOLWA

Burgess, Rev. H. J., Cyclopedia of South Australia, *Vol. 2, 1909.*

Colley, R. B., Port Elliot and Goolwa, Inman Valley.

James, H. R., & Co., South Australia, Premier Watering Resort, *1928.*

Proud, G., Murray and Darling Trade, *1883.*

Hodge, C. R., Encounter Bay, The Miniature Naples of Australia, *1932.*

YORK

Hammond, Y. E., Western Pioneers.

COOLGARDIE

Back to Goldfields Carnival, 1927.

Calvert, A. T., My fourth tour in Western Australia, *1897.*

Ford, W., Coolgardie in 1892.

The Golden Age—A Collection of Newspaper Cuttings, 1894–7. Mitchell Library Collection.

Kirwan, Sir Y. W., Early Gold Field Days, *Vol. 3.*

Marshall, I., Battling for Gold.

Compton, Y. S., Coolgardie: Christmas at the Old Camp, Kalgoorlie, *Kalgoorlie 1959.*

Reid, A., Those were the Days, *1933.*

Reside, W. J., Golden Days, *1921.*

Stoddart, J., Early days of Coolgardie, *Western Australia Historical Society, Journal and Proceedings, Vol. 1, 1930.*

Uren, M., Glint of Gold, *Melbourne, R. & M., 1948.*

BROOME

Dampier Despatch No. 66, 69. John B. Hughes.

Durack, M., Time and Tide.

Edmonds, W. D., Story of Air Forces.

Healy, T. & A., And Far from Home, *1936.*

Hill, Ernestine, Great Australian Loneliness.

Holmes, C. H., We find Australia, *1933.*

Idriess, I. L., Forty Fathoms Deep.

Kornitzer, Trade Winds, *1933.*

Sawden, W. J., With the Nor'west Trail, *1903.*

CHARTERS TOWERS

W. Clowes & Sons, Charters Towers Gold Fields, Its Rise and Progress, *London, issued for*
W. Clowes & Sons, 1886.

British India and Queensland Agency Co., Handbook, *1886.*

Harrison Printing Company, Central Western and Northern Queensland Today, *1914.*

Irviney, A. J., Mining and Descriptive Queensland, *1889.*

Lees, W., Gold Fields in Queensland, *1889, Mitchell Library Collection.*

Marsland, L. W., Charters Towers Town and Gold Fields, *1892.*

Parker, Sir Y., Round the Compass in Australia, *1892.*

RAVENSWOOD

Queensland Government Mining Journal 1901: *Special number for the Glasgow International*
Exhibition.

Weitemeyer, T. P., Missing Friends, *1892, Mitchell Library Collection*

Hurle, H. H. C., Discovery of the Ravenswood Gold Fields, *Historical Society Queensland*
   Journal, Vol. 1, 1919.

CHILDERS

Eadie's Illustrated Bundaberg Almanac for 1909.

Childer, S., The Life and Correspondence of Rt. Hon. C. E. Childers, 1827–1896, *London,*
   Murray, 1901.

Thomson, I., The Sum of our Yesterdays: A reference to 85 years settlement in the Isis district to
   1964. *Isis Publishing Co., Childers.*

NORMANTON

British India and Queensland Agency Co., Handbook of Information for the Colonies and India,
   1897–1898.

Cowl, T. H., Experiences travelling to and three years residence in Normanton, *Mitchell*
   Libary Collection, 1919.

Palmer, E., Early Days in Northern Queensland.

General Bibliography

Rose, A. J., Patterns of Cities, *Nelson, 1967.*

Jeans, D. N., An historical geography of New South Wales to 1901, *Reed Education, 1972.*

Summerson, J., Georgian London, *Barrie & Jenkins, 1945.*

Brain, A. J., & Sherrard, H. M., Town and Country Planning, *Melbourne University Press, 1951.*

Mumford, L., The City in History, *Pelican, 1961.*

Sharp, T., The Anatomy of the Village, *Penguin, 1946.*

Winstan, D., Sydney's Great Experiment.

Sulman, J., Town Planning in Australia.

12921